TRAVELS AND TRIBULATIONS

To Mom

I tried my best to recreate events, locations and conversations from my memories of them. In order to protect people's privacy, in some instances I have changed the names of individuals and places, some identifying characteristics and details such as physical features, occupations and places of residence.

Copyeditor: Andra Bosneag
Proofreader: Alyssa Nelson
Interior Design: Tyrel Nelson
Front cover photo: © Alyssa Nelson
Author photo: © Alyssa Nelson

CONTENTS

Mom and me, Blaine, Minnesota, August 2002. Photo by Jay T. Nelson.

Introduction

I could hear laughter rolling toward my side of the gym. Curious, I turned to learn that I was the reason why a circle of eighth-grade classmates was chuckling at midcourt.

"There's the dude with my Gophers shirt," the ringleader sneered. He was pointing right at me.

I didn't know who he was since I was new to the school. Yet I knew how he recognized my attire. My mother had recently purchased the crew neck at an area thrift store; that's where a lot of my brother's and my clothes came from. In fact, the jersey she bought advertised the previous season's basketball camp at the University of Minnesota, which made it identifiable to anybody who attended. Moreover, there was a lone player autograph that stretched across the shoulder blades. Whoever donated the tee would immediately remember its distinct signature. The John Hancock might as well have been a beacon.

I was mortified. I initially thought it made sense to sport the shirt to tryouts, but I instantly regretted this choice. It wouldn't be a difficult decision for the coaches either because I basically psyched myself out.

"Bastards!" Mom exclaimed upon listening to my embarrassing story.

"To hell with them!" Dad added.

It was no shock that my parents, who were extremely comfortable in their own skin, had such responses. My typical reaction during my adolescence, however, was to protect myself. So I was determined to deny that my duds were secondhand. And I certainly didn't reveal where I dwelled unless I absolutely trusted the person. Growing up in a couple of trailer parks made me a target for teasing.

Looking back, I wish I would have stood up for myself more when I was treated like crap for simply being from a low-income household. If I could go back, I'd confront the haters head-on. I would own where I came from and say how proud I was of my family. The only excuse I have for not doing so is the insecurity inherent in being a youngster. I definitely can't blame my parents.

Although I may have lacked some material items, my mom and pop instilled in me values for which I am now forever grateful. They displayed self-confidence. In truth, they always walked tall and never omitted where they came from. They were selfless, ceaselessly caring for others more than themselves. Mom often lent the little spending money she had to neighbors in need, and Dad once knowingly wrote a bad check at the grocery store so my brother and I could have dinner that evening. My parents also encouraged me to reach for the highs. They urged me to shoot big, to do things while I can since time is not guaranteed, which explains why they wholeheartedly supported my globetrotting. And my parents showed me how to live through the lows of losing someone close. Despite blow after devastating blow, I witnessed them fiercely press on during the few decades I shared with them.

A handful of months after my mother departed to meet my father beyond the pearly gates, I engaged in a long conversation with an area contractor. My background and international volunteering eventually surfaced. Realizing that I resided in a double-wide on the opposite side of the freeway from his childhood abode, he appeared surprised.

"How does a trailer park kid end up seeing the world and helping people?" he asked.

I was a tad bemused by his question. I didn't understand how being raised in a mobile home had any relevance, yet my answer was easy.

"I had awesome parents," I replied.

Soon after that summer chat, I began working on this book—a collection of previously published alongside some unreleased narratives. To be honest, I had time. I had just been laid off. And due to the COVID-19 pandemic, I was searching for ways to keep myself from banging my head against the walls of my rambler when I couldn't escape outdoors for a bit. Losing my second parent pushed me into persistent pensiveness, too. Day in, day out, I found myself jumping with the ups and depressed about the downs I had experienced over the past several years. I wanted to share this seesaw of sentiments, especially because the principles— honor in one's origins, compassion, living in the moment, resiliency—my mom and pop gifted me are present in these pages.

The upcoming chapters encapsulate a ride of a dozen years, starting in 2008 and finishing in 2020—from my late twenties to my early forties. The physical excursions climb the Ecuadorian Andes, stroll through surveys at sea level, and descend into Guatemalan lowlands. The emotional journeys soar with my spirits at certain points and dive into the depths of my despair at others. Whether they are literal or spiritual, I believe the following travels and tribulations not only depict how I ended up seeing my world but also how people helped open my eyes to it.

1

Coming Around to Carnival

It was the end of January, and I didn't trust a soul. Elderly, green, male, or female, I was suspicious of everybody I saw in Cuenca. No matter how innocent they looked, I could nonetheless imagine the *cuencanos* launching an aqua grenade or aiming a plastic pistol at me without warning. I was sick of Carnival. I was tired of keeping my skull on a swivel when I was outside the dry confines of my apartment.

However, I felt a tad better upon seeing that both foreigners and Ecuadorians were considered fair game. Yet I still wasn't a fan of water-throwing. Continuously in search of methods to avoid the wetness, I eventually heard about a potential refuge from the deluge. Far different from how the rest of the country experienced the Pre-Lenten Season, the tradition of water-throwing was prohibited in downtown Ambato—seven hours away by *autobús*.

In truth, the Andean town was famous for scrapping squirt guns, buckets, and balloons during the annual festival. The *ambateños*, therefore, compensated for this enforced lack of liquid by dousing their targets with aerosol cans full of colorful, scented foam known as *carioca*. But I was OK with carioca. I was willing to risk being caked with suds up north rather than suffer one more water bomb assault on the sidewalks of Cuenca. And when Andrew, my amigo from Loja (a calm municipality near Ecuador's southern tip), informed me he was visiting Ambato, I instantly agreed to meet him there.

An eternity on a swerving, nauseating coach brought me to the hub of the Tungurahua Province. I groggily debussed to join Andrew for lunch in the main plaza. Once restored to walking order, we wandered to the southern outskirts. We climbed numerous stairs to a littered lookout, which was loitered by a lone local. Observing the active streets below, my fellow English teacher and I were in the midst of describing our new homes and jobs when something shiny abruptly caught my attention.

I squinted at a tall, jagged sculpture protruding from the polar end of the valley. The giant metallic shard stabbed the February sky. Though it was a peculiar piece of architecture, I was more intrigued by how the enormous silver shank appeared to be on the one piece of earth higher than ours.

"¿Cómo se llama aquel mirador?" I asked the gent to my left. *What's the name of that viewpoint over there?*

"Es el Monumento a la Primera Imprenta," he replied. *It's the Monument to the First Printing Press.*

"¿Cómo llegamos allá?" I heard Andrew inquire on my right. *How do we get there?*

"Sígan la Juan Montalvo hasta que crucen el río," the man responded. *Follow Juan Montalvo until you cross the river.* "Pueden subir el cerro por allá." *You can climb the hill over there.*

As the rays faded from the Central Sierra basin, our tour guide for the moment nodded to the top landmarks and barrios. He also informed us of the best Carnival events, like the Fruit and Flowers Parade and scheduled bullfights. We were nonetheless short on sun and would have to dine with some old friends in a bit. So we wished our acquaintance well. We decided to save the First Printing Press for another time.

Andrew and I began Saturday evening catching up with Liz, Nick, Nicole, and Rozana, our peers who had arrived by means of a three-hour bus ride from the north. The six of us were TESOL (Teaching English to Speakers of Other Languages) schoolmates in Quito just four months earlier. This was our first reunion since Andrew left for Loja, and I moved to Cuenca immediately upon finishing the 130-hour course—our ten classmates stayed in the capital to work.

Later, while our four pals were enjoying an Aventura concert, Andrew and I spent the remainder of the night patrolling Avenida Pedro Fermin Cevallos, spraying carioca back at those who provoked us. In fact, we developed a solid system of retribution. If one of us was hit, the attacker was promptly double-teamed. The four-lane byway was packed, too. Individuals of varying ages and nationalities discharged perfumed foam on foot, out of pickup beds, and from the interiors of trolling vehicles. People in all directions carried out solo missions, worked in pairs, or swaggered in tin-flaunting gangs. I'd never seen such chaos before.

It was mutual madness. The vast majority of those on Cevallos accepted that they were going to wind up rainbow-colored and smelling like a florist. It was actually a lot of fun letting loose in the sudsy free-for-all. The frothy vendors made a bundle off Andrew and me. Except for getting carioca in the eyes or mouth every now and then, partaking in this unique fiesta was well worth a couple bucks per can.

After spending Sunday watching the Fruit and Flowers Parade, not to mention a bullfight with our Quito colleagues, Andrew and I found ourselves completing the task we had set on Saturday afternoon. Although we got lost in a maze of manors, we ultimately located the right trail on the wrong side of the tracks. We passed many humbler abodes and a decrepit bullpen on the rise to the bull's eye. Finally, we reached the sculpture which had lured us from the opposing edge of the valley two days prior.

The Monday morning cloud cover chilled our bones while we shook our heads at the graffiti-riddled monument. The remnants of last night's fireworks display decorated the circular cement platform. We snapped various panoramas in order to capture the gloomy pueblo in its entirety. The eerie silence of the site made it seem as if we were alone in the canton.

As my *compañero* continued to shoot photos, I realized my recent change in attitude. Despite my initial dislike of the celebration, Ambato had shown me a positive aspect of Carnival. I pictured myself back on Cevallos, in the thick of the carioca fight, and having a blast. Everyone was all in, including me. Suddenly, Andrew awakened me from my daze.

"I'm done!" he shouted. "What now?"

I couldn't answer his question. Despite getting our photo fix, it was clear the two of us weren't satisfied. We were bored, it was hardly midday, and Carnival wasn't over.

With this in mind, my accomplice raised an excellent point: we still had a couple cans of foam at the hotel.

2

Death in Another Light

There wasn't a cloud over the Pacific. Drinking my black coffee atop Hotel La Cabaña, I couldn't take my eyes off the skies. The incoming bay breezes were quite invigorating. It was a picturesque morning in Puerto Ángel, Oaxaca.

Suddenly, an unexpected question brought me back to the girl with whom I'd been chatting.

"¿Qué piensan los estadounidenses de la muerte?" asked Tanya, before sipping from her cup of Joe. *What do Americans think about death?*

"Creo que la mayoría tiene miedo a morir," I replied. *I believe most are scared of dying.* "¿Qué piensas tú?" *What do you think?*

"En México, vemos la muerte como parte del ciclo de vida." *In Mexico, we see death as part of the life cycle.*

"Entonces, ¿no la toman en serio?" *So, you don't take it seriously?*

"Nos divertimos en vida y en muerte," Tanya explained while her brown peepers focused on something behind me. *We have fun in life and in death.*

I peeked over my shoulder and spotted what had triggered this topic. Below the railing of our thatched rooftop was a splendid *cementerio*. I was immediately impressed with the vibrant graves and endless crucifixes which dominated the healthy hillside.

"Es bello," I said. *It's beautiful.*

"Así es. Deberías entrar," the Cuernavaca native suggested. *It is. You should go inside.*

I agreed. During the next half hour, the conversation changed to other subjects, like Gabriel García Márquez and rock music. But I still couldn't get that marble town out of my mind. I would have to investigate further.

I found myself eagerly approaching death's door a few days later. I had been anxious to tour the tombs ever since Tanya's recommendation, but it wasn't the actual reason for my perspiration. The February sun was searing, causing my pack to stick to my soaked back. Despite the sweat stinging my eyes, I was nonetheless set on what lurked beyond the cyan archway. I wiped my brow with a sopping bandana and entered the cemetery.

Although I was meandering amongst the dead, the verdant slope was very much alive due to its vistas, alluring adornments, and sharp colors. The funerary grounds provided an excellent view of the ocean waves which quietly flowed in from the Bahía de Puerto Ángel and lightly splashed upon Playa Panteón. The tombs were delightfully decorated as well. Countless candles, infinite flowers, and glossy black pottery rested on the resting places. Sparkling white, striking yellow, and stunning blue hues also enriched the walkabout.

Intrigued by the stillness of the site, I carefully snaked upward. I took stock in utter serenity, constantly weaving around leafy trees and shrubs to photograph the comely crypts

Puerto Ángel, Oaxaca, Mexico, February 2009

in my path. The dead air made me feel like I was the only person in the world while I ascended the hill. I finally reached the crest and ogled the cementerio for what seemed an eternity. I admired Puerto Ángel's charming cove as I caught my breath. With a second wind at last, I enjoyed the Pacific gusts sweeping across my face before eventually hiking back down.

Descending through the deceased, I saw a middle-aged man dusting off a handful of headstones near the exit. I noticed he was watching me from under the weathered brim of his brown cowboy hat. However, the guy didn't say a thing. He simply nodded and grinned.

Oddly enough, I got it; no words were needed. I understood that his smile was mirroring mine. The fellow's silent pleasantry was rather appropriate to boot. It represented the silent pleasantness I had just experienced in the graveyard. And when I squinted at the sun blazing high above the cemetery gates, I also realized that death never looked so bright.

Cemetery, Puerto Ángel, Oaxaca, Mexico, February 2009

3

Views of Vizcaya

It's me, the trees, and Juan Ponce de León. Never before did I think I'd be face-to-face with such a famous man during my Florida vacation. Not only was he Puerto Rico's first governor, but he also named the state beneath my feet. I'm not starstruck though … perhaps because I'm on the verge of heat stroke.

The lid of the Miami morning is intense; the sky practically white it is so bright. And the mid-August air is heavy, almost forcing me to fall at the boots of the towering Spanish explorer.

Glancing left, my parched jaw drops at the sight of an awesome concrete structure. It seems out of place—an Italian look in a subtropical backdrop. Yet Juan's stare remains stone cold. Maybe he is disappointed. While we're on touristic terrain, we aren't at the legendary, albeit undiscovered, Fountain of Youth attached to Ponce de León's bio. Excited to explore Vizcaya—the winter estate of industrialist James Deering—I opt to move on sans Juan. He is a statue after all.

I enter the museum which, in spite of its centuries-old appearance, was actually completed in 1916. I'm immediately fascinated by the courtyard. It is immersed in sunlight and surrounded by flourishing flora. Inching along the first and second floors, I study the antique European and American décor (ranging from the 1400s to the 1800s) displayed throughout the mansion. Among the thirty-plus rooms are an elegant sitting area, a tea niche with stained glass windows, and an intimate music space that one sees in movies akin to *Pride and Prejudice.* It has a piano, harp, and even a dulcimer.

At the same time, I am intrigued by the home's technologies, which are well-advanced for the early twentieth century. For instance, there is an elevator, telephone nook, and lavatories modern enough to compete with today's standards. My favorite parts of the manor are its spiral stairway, the dumbwaiter linking the kitchen and butler's pantry, and the bookshelf in the library that doubles as a disguised entrance to the reception. Notwithstanding these unique features, the crannies are countless, and I am beginning to feel claustrophobic. I bolt to the marbled East Loggia and open the big glass doors.

Accessing the East Terrace, I am introduced to the Floridian surf. But much of my view of Biscayne Bay is obstructed by a rock ship ("Barge") serving as a breaker. I ignore the boat landing located at the northern limits of Vizcaya's inlet and shuffle to the quaint, plein-air teahouse on the opposite side. Tall teal windows circle me. There are mangroves swamping the shoreline gaps. I turn to the sea. The Atlantic waters are pacific. The sound is silent. Ogling the ocean for a bit, I head for the formal fields.

The southerly acreage is vast. Taking a deep breath, I embark on the eastern edge, eager to eyeball the mixture of Renaissance French and Italian architecture framing the grounds. My first stop is the Secret Garden. I especially like the jagged cavern hiding between the two staircases to the west, not to mention the lengthy scarlet leaves of the shrubs bordering the steps. Next, I rest in the shade of the branches covering the East Statuary Walk. Wiping the sweat off my aviators, I admire a pair of white marble sphinxes facing the unclosed gate of the Theater Garden. I wander inside and visit the metallic, intricately carved shepherd and shepherdess protecting the peaceful enclosure. The Fountain Garden then engages my attention. Despite being bone dry (due to renovation), I am still impressed by the yard's bull's-eye: a grand bubbler at the center of a ring of stoic sculptures. Moreover, the plot's bright green plants and lawns provide a striking contrast to the dark mangroves wildly looming behind. So do my beet red cheeks. I saunter to the southern tip of the premises.

Secret Garden, Vizcaya Museum and Gardens, Miami, Florida, August 2011

I climb a gritty set of stairs. There I find the Casino, a two-roomed edifice exposed to the elements. Reaching for the iron railing of the balcony, I catch my breath while examining the pavilion's ornate columns. I am transfixed by what I notice next.

Leaving the Casino, I lean into the light to check out an all-encompassing vista of the property from the top of the Mound. Below are brilliant cascades and grottos. Just beyond them is a charming central island moated by a tranquil pool. The sight of the water, however, makes my thirst even worse. I smack my lips.

I wend west. Like I did their eastern counterparts, I contemplate the carvings on this end of the grounds. My concentration then shifts to the verdant environs of the West Statuary Walk. I am drawn to the labyrinth of dense bushes, vines, and trees. Plodding past more flowers and fountains, I rubberneck the depths of the rockland hammock—a forest far different from those of the oaks back in Minnesota—the entire way to the exit.

Sighing and sopping, I drag myself toward the rental car. I stop to bid Ponce de León adieu. I question his quest for immortality and whether half a millennium ago he stood where he stands now. And if so, I wonder what he saw. I turn around to gain perspective.

Taking in Vizcaya one last time, I don't blame Ponce for pulling up here. Although he never came across the Fountain of Youth, he found something magical nonetheless.

Descent to the Fountain Garden, Vizcaya Museum and Gardens, Miami, Florida, August 2011

4

Flashbacks, Fear, and Flamingos

It's the summer of 1987. I am on a family vacation in Wisconsin Dells. My little brother Jay, who is merely six, is beside himself next to my parents' boat, the Mercury Grand Marquis. He is bawling—his tears full of fear. My mom rushes to him on the edge of the parking lot, not only to provide comfort but to avoid the ominous threshold of the haunted house as well. The fright on their faces undoubtedly scares me, too. I turn to join them when I am yanked into the dark without warning. There was no way my dad was going to let two wasted tickets become three.

What occurs next is a shadowy blur. In truth, I have no recollection of the actual interior of the haunted house. All I recall is Pop's firm grip, his pissed-off pace, and that I continuously cried, "I wanna go home!"

A quarter-century later, I am contemplating another eerie entrance. I'm without the fam on this occasion, visiting the Sunshine State rather than America's Dairyland. Even though I'm much older now, part of me remains the eight-year-old who's afraid to proceed. I take a deep breath. My shaky hand grabs the metal handle, and I cautiously step inside. I want to take flight the second the creaky door closes.

I'm instantly in a Hitchcock film. Several birds circle just above me. I hunch. Others waddle uncomfortably close; their dead eyes cause mine to bulge. They close in. I back up. A cacophony of caws, cackles, and cries raise my hair on end. Their shrills are unsettling, and my heart is racing! I desperately reach for the handle. I clench it. Spinning around, I pull with everything I have. I run! The door slams behind me. WHAM! I don't dare glance over my shoulder.

Composing myself, I appreciate the sudden silence. I gaze at the palms, exotic plants, and vines dangling directly in front of me. I can't believe I'm in Davie, Florida, exploring the

Flamingo Gardens—a nonprofit arboretum and wildlife refuge west of Ft. Lauderdale—and not the Amazon. I further wonder if anyone has ever toured all 25,000 square feet of the Everglades Free-flight Aviary I just fled. A soul much braver than me, I decide. Wishing what lies ahead to be easier on the nerves, I venture into the boscage, thinking of the last time I was alarmed by animals.

It's the spring of 2007. I'm on a Habitat for Humanity trip in La Ceiba, Honduras. After getting a beer, my co-leader Val and I start for our hotel. We are in the middle of the street in the middle of the night when a couple of Doberman pinschers abruptly roadblock us. They're foaming at the mouth. They snarl viciously. The watchdogs then pounce, ferociously barking the entire time. Val and I frenziedly backpedal down the empty avenue. While retreating, we also wind up, wildly pretending to throw rocks—a futile tip we had recently heard—at our enemies. But our fast-approaching attackers aren't fazed in the slightest. So we opt to drop the imaginary stones in order to protect ourselves, putting our arms up in the style of boxers on the defense. We frantically fall back until, for some reason I still fail to comprehend, the dogs unexpectedly pull up. It was as if they ran into an invisible fence. Perplexed and grateful to be intact, Val and I bolt for the inn like mutts with two tails.

Refocusing on the nature reserve, I bird-dog the upcoming trail. I copy a cat on eggshells while a tabby stares at me. It ogles me for a bit before wandering into the thicket.

Flamingo Gardens, Davie, Florida, August 2011

Sunlight occasionally pierces the dank hammock. A musty odor fills the air. I constantly swat away bugs. The swerving track leads me through a labyrinth of overgrown ferns, towering oaks, and bright orchids. I stop frequently to investigate my jungly surroundings … and to pluck the webs from my sweaty face. I notice one of the arachnids which spun endless strands looming above. The black and yellow spider looks bigger than my camera. My anxiety from the aviary immediately returns. I pick up the pace.

Peacocks cross my path until I spot pink flamingos and white ibises. These birds are much calmer than those I saw earlier. In fact, they don't care I'm there. They simply go about their business, posing by the pond.

With tiny iguanas scampering along the walk, I visit a much bigger reptile. I amble by the Alligator Lagoon. The sole occupant is clearly beaten by the heat, searching for cover somewhere on the bottom of its shallow cement pool.

Next, I observe freshwater turtles of many designs and sizes. They gawk at me with their wide-open peepers. I happen upon a tortoise to boot. The recluse, however, seems more interested in the underbrush than anything else.

I finally board the tram. Its Easter colors leap out from the woodsy background. The ride is sporadic, either furiously zigzagging for stretches or creeping across the terrain. I'm in awe of the varied landscape as a man with a mic describes the wetlands, citrus groves, and rainforest slapping against the turquoise railings and pink roofs of the trolley cars. And I listen intently while he talks about the sanctuary's sixteen Champion trees. These sixty hidden acres are unique indeed.

I exit the tram around a half hour later. The guide informs me that one of the panthers in the nearby exhibit is visible. I press my mug on the glass. I scan for a few minutes before locating Florida's state animal. The feline is nestled in the tall grass beneath a shade tree, enjoying a siesta.

Worn out from the day, I promptly head for the hotel. It's time for me to do the same.

5

Lake Reflections

I exit the hardware store with new work gloves in hand. I immediately slip them onto my numbing fingers. The wind of the gloomy February afternoon picks up as I hustle to my pickup. The Minnesota winter is stinging, and I can't wait to return to the warm confines of home.

I fire up the Ford. Setting the heat to high, I can't ignore the pier a few hundred yards away. It's a recognizable sight, a site I have driven by hundreds of times over the years, but haven't visited in decades. While the whipping gales rock the Ranger like a bobblehead, I stare through my windshield, wondering why I'm now being drawn to the water. I shift into first.

A forlorn feeling fills my cab as I approach the loch. Sporadic groups of trees and dead cattails decorate its desolate shores. Two crows circle high above; the only animals to be seen. Not a soul is ice fishing. Nor is there anyone on the lonely trail surrounding the mere. Though the lake is within a stone's throw of the local airport, it is the bluest lagoon I have ever laid eyes on. I park in the empty lot.

It takes just a couple of paces to jog my memory. I notice an opening in the cattails, a clearing perfect for boatless anglers. Familiarity lures me to the fishing spot. I know I have been here before. However, I can't determine when. Studying the various sets of footsteps atop the ice, I retrace my own. For minutes, I scroll through the pictures in my head. I stop at an image from almost thirty years ago.

I'm only four or five. I cast my line and … WHOOM! The tug is incredible, practically ripping the pole out of my tiny fins. I somehow manage to hang on. Chomping at the bit, I reel and reel to no avail.

Despite my valiant effort, I can't bring in the beast. The tables seem to be turned—I'm actually being yanked in. Yet I don't let go; I keep cranking and cranking. The shallows are up to my waist. I hear a thunderous noise from behind.

SPLASH! SPLASH! SPLASH! SPLASH! SPLASH! Two Popeye-like forearms instantly appear around mine. The pull from the abyss weakens. The rod is nearly vertical. And the sea monster (a large northern in reality) is ultimately brought to the surface. I am mesmerized by its cold black peepers while it angrily dangles above the ripples.

We're soon beached on the beach. My proud father is kneeling, wrapping the pike in his T-shirt. He's in his prime: young, strong, and full of life. He looks up at me. His bearded grin is ear-to-ear. The flashback fades.

Tears are streaming down my face. I realize it has been over a year since I last saw Dad smile. Today is February 20, 2012. My pop died on Valentine's Day last year. I resume my stroll, saddened by this truth.

The path leads me to more reminders of my childhood. Verging on the dock, I recall painstakingly placing my feet on its wooden planks, terrified of falling between the cracks, and watching an elderly fellow hook a huge snapper from the end of the platform. The turtle flails its limbs during its emergence from the weeds.

Taft Lake, Richfield, Minnesota, February 2012

On a trailside bench, I remember my old man approaching a pair of anglers in need. The dudes appear to be in their twenties, and one is trying to delicately remove the multi-pronged lure deeply entrenched in his pal's cheek. Although the victim is surprisingly quiet, his mug advertises agony. My father regretfully concludes there is nothing he can do. He promptly suggests the guys go to the ER.

In fact, I can almost see the VA Medical Center from here. I naturally reflect on the daze surrounding my dad's cancer diagnosis. I think of our chats in his hospital room. I replay one heart-to-heart in particular.

"Jay's handling this better than me," I admit.

"Your brother's tough; not much gets to him," Pop replies.

"That's for sure. I'm way more emotional than he is."

"Yeah, but it's also good to be emotional. And you're pretty tough too, Tyrel."

I sigh. I miss my father's boosts of confidence. I miss his love.

Nevertheless, I am comforted by this walk along Memory Lake. I am convinced Dad has drawn me to the water—a childhood scene which has opened a floodgate of recollections—to show he's still looking after me. I close my eyes. He's beaming down upon me.

I gaze at the heavens as I round the final bend in the shoreline. I believe my pop is watching me from somewhere beyond the passing planes. While I can't see him, I have faith I will someday; just not on this plain.

6

Forging Through the Fourth

Spending all day indoors is unbearable for me during the summer. Whether the weather is fair or feverish, I have to the maximize my free time outside the house. So I bug Alyssa to do something outdoors until she can no longer put up with my hyperactivity. In addition, my number one volunteers to drive because she'll surely make it to our destination faster, which means the faster I'll get these ants out of my pants. I even have the perfect place in mind. She just has no idea where it is.

"Where is it, Ty?"

"Hang a left here."

"I only see trees!"

"Turn left!"

Alyssa jerks the wheel counterclockwise. She veers onto a narrow road leading to a paved clearing. She parks on the far edge of the vacant asphalt.

"I didn't know this place was here! I drove right past it a couple months ago."

"I bet tons of people miss it," I say while noting the endless foliage consuming the area.

"How do you know about it?"

"I was driving around bored last year and found it by accident."

We step out of the Sonata and into an oven. The humidity instantly smacks me in the face. Certain my eyes will soon sting if I don't act immediately, I grab my baseball cap from the backseat. Rather than a headband or bandana, I prefer a hat to absorb my overabundant perspiration. I remove my shades and set them on the dash; they'll fog up. I pull my visor down as low as possible to block the fiery sun.

"The sky looks hazy, smoggy like Los Angeles," my better half observes.

I squint across the hood of the Hyundai to catch Alyssa ogling the heavens. She wipes her brow with the back of her hand. She slings her camera over her shoulder. I follow suit. We take last-second gulps from our water bottles. Matching each other stride for stride, we plod across the empty lot—our gaits already heavy from the weight of the soggy skies.

Dead air drapes over Bloomington, Minnesota. We are speechless, awestruck by the silence of the refuge. Our footsteps seem unusually loud while they crunch the unpaved trail. A fly buzzes by every now and then. A branch occasionally whines in the wind. We enter the Hyland Lake Park Reserve sole survivors of the Apocalypse.

In reality, most people are probably hiding from the heat. I picture them curled up beside their floor registers with their ACs cranked. The temperature has hit 101° in the Twin Cities, a record for July 4. And since it's Independence Day, our fellow humans are either out of town or waiting inside till the fireworks fire off. It will be cooler then, temp-wise and aesthetically.

The animals are apparently holed up, too. As we tour the reserve, Alyssa and I notice the marshes are motionless; the lagoons resemble paintings due to their lack of ripples. We spot no muskrats at Muskrat Pond, no wood ducks at Wood Duck Pond, and no turtles basking at the Turtle Basking Pond. But just when we assume we're alone, we realize the contrary.

Hyland Lake Park Reserve, Bloomington, Minnesota, July 2012

Ascending the Aspen Trail, we sense we're being watched. We abruptly stop on the woodchips. Scanning the vegetation, we locate a duo of turkeys poking their heads through the brush like a pair of periscopes. They're beady black peepers fix on us. They gape for several seconds, turn, and run off to tell their friends.

From this point forward, we can't go more than a moment or two without staredowns with fowl. They prove to be harmless, though. The turkeys scamper off the path whenever we get close, clearly not wanting to play chicken. I conclude they're simply intrigued to witness a couple of crazies actually trudging in this torridity.

Batty or not, we proceed through the swelter. We reach the Oak Trail. Thankfully, the thick canopy of this three-quarter-mile stretch provides long periods of shade, allowing us to recharge a bit. The leafy tunnel is captivating. Red berries and lavender flowers decorate the dense green wall. Marveling at the monstrous heights and widths of the trees, we are also fascinated by their snakelike branches. They twist, turn, and fork forever.

Emerging from the oak forest, we happen upon a wide-open prairie. Documentaries of the Serengeti come to mind while I study the vast grassland. I envision zebras and gazelles darting across the plain's long and winding road. I gaze into the distant woods enclosing the suburban savanna. Mesmerized by the swaying trunks, I listen intently. I hear no traffic from 494—one of the state's busiest highways, which is a stone's throw to the north.

Instead, a light breeze rustles the treetops, producing a calming white noise similar to rainfall. The lull of this hidden metropolitan sanctuary makes it hard to believe that the airport and Mall of America are only a few miles east. Taking in the serene landscape, I notice Alyssa's ponytail bobbing far down the trail. I pick up my pace.

We're at the entrance of Richardson Nature Center a little later. Feeling a cool mist blow, we yank on the tall glass doors. We rush inside to absorb the air conditioning. Central air has never felt so refreshing.

A survey of the building shows vibrant clay mosaics adorning exhibit walls. Books, pamphlets, and maps decorate the shelves. We further learn that there are indeed more animals at the nature center—aquariums housing snakes and turtles, to be exact. We approach the reptiles for a closer inspection.

A false map turtle follows Alyssa's pointer finger back and forth across the glass of its tank. Suddenly, I hear paperwork. I pursue the shuffling around a large staircase. I find a woman sitting behind an info desk.

"Hello!" she greets cheerfully.

"Hi!" I reply, somewhat startled.

"The park is all yours!" the bespectacled lady offers, obviously thinking we've just arrived.

"Yeah, there's no one else here," Alyssa responds over my shoulder.

"Isn't this heat awful?" the employee asks.

My partner and I nod simultaneously.

"Well, be careful out there. You two enjoy your day!"

We leave the lobby figuring we've already accomplished this. Before exiting, however, we make a discovery which tops off the afternoon: a pair of chilled water fountains. We guzzle copious amounts of ice cold H20 prior to returning to the sultriness.

We drag ourselves across the pavement and finally reach the car. The interior roasting, we stand for a bit with the doors open.

"Are you palpitating?" Alyssa inquires.

"Yup," I reply, tapping my right hand on my heart.

"That's because you're dehydrated."

"I'll be fine."

She shoots me a concerned look, yet I look past it. I home in on the trailhead on the opposite side of the lot.

"Where does that path go?"

Alyssa doesn't even turn to acknowledge what I'm referring to.

"Another day, honey," she answers. "I'm too hot."

Three Rivers Park District, Hennepin County, Minnesota, July 2012

7

Autumn in August

I am fluttering like a streamer attached to a fan. A fan, however, is the last thing I need right now. I grab at the Ranger's console to crank the heat. Hot air fills the Ford, yet goosebumps keep popping on my skin. I yank my cap down to my brows. I fold my arms. Checking my pickup's mirrors to view if anyone picks up on my delirium, I realize the other cars at the intersection have their windows closed. The only difference is that they're running their ACs. It is mid-August after all, and the temp is nearly ninety degrees.

Clenching the wheel to stabilize my shivering body, I squint at the red light dangling overhead. I shove the gearshift into first as soon as the signal changes. I practically stomp the gas pedal past the floor. The rest of the ride home is a blur.

"It sounds like the ocean!"

Refocusing on the present, I see Alyssa is transfixed by the swaying trees of the Murphy-Hanrehan Reserve. She, too, is enjoying the summer breeze blowing across Savage, Minnesota. The current steadily rustles the branches, creating a hypnotic white noise which could easily lull those within earshot into a daydream.

"Yup, sounds exactly the same," I sigh in response.

I am grateful to be back in the thicket instead of reliving such a dreadful commute. I have nonetheless failed to shake the shakes of that feverish Friday. In fact, that bedridden weekend has weakened me; I am still winded a fortnight later. Come what may, the lullaby of the park has thus far made today's bullheaded choice to force myself outdoors worthwhile.

But the woodland's soothing gusts aren't the lone element we take in. We're hardly beyond the entrance when we discover that the leaves are beginning to turn, even though three weeks remain until the official arrival of autumn. Dead petals litter the beaten path as warm hues poke through the greenery. Alyssa, who loves the fall, is pleased by the season's apparent head start.

"Autumn in August!" she exclaims. "There's a title for you!"

"It's actually September 1."

"You know it looked like this yesterday."

"Nope, don't think so," I say with a smirk.

Alyssa smiles and predictably rolls her eyes. We wander onward, wondering what additional surprises the forest has in store for us.

We notice the glow immediately. Absorbing the bright rays of the late afternoon sun, the thick canopy luminesces above. The distinct color produced by some sections of the foliage reminds me of glow sticks. I envision the tiny stars shining from the ceiling of my childhood bedroom at night.

Traversing the dense refuge, Alyssa and I catch sporadic glimpses of secluded ponds. We spot various mushrooms protruding from trailside trunks. And the trees lean in every direction—many of their branches curl like twist ties. The pathway proves to be interesting in and of itself. Not only does the route wend up and down steep hills, but it also leads us to flat stretches laden with acorns. The track even transforms into a weathered boardwalk lined with cattails, which cuts across the middle of low-lying marshes.

Murphy-Hanrehan Park Reserve, Savage, Minnesota, September 2012

While I wheeze and whine through the woods, my partner ambles at my slothful pace, constantly checking on me.

"We probably should've stayed home," Alyssa admits. "You need to rest."

"Yeah, I know," I reply. "I'm tired of being cooped up, though."

"You're so stubborn!"

About ninety minutes pass when we find ourselves back at the front. Studying a map posted near the parking lot, we learn we have merely toured the tip of the iceberg, or rather the northern tip of the reserve. The grid shows umpteen miles of unpaved tracks which snake to the south. Nevertheless, I can't see another tree. I am bushed.

"We'll come back," Alyssa quickly decides, noting my shortness in breath. "How are you doing?"

"Not too bad," I respond, following a series of coughs. "You're driving home, right?"

"Of course, Mister."

I hand Alyssa the keys while crossing the dusty lot. She fires up the Hyundai, and I slouch in the passenger seat.

I turn the radio dial to the Minnesota Twins game. Listening to America's favorite pastime strangely reminds me of my childhood illnesses. In truth, for much of my youth, it was a given: I was going to get sick within the first few months of the year. From elementary to high school, I spent dozens of days on the couch, shivering under a stack of blankets, and hoping I'd recover before baseball started. Some springs, I regained my health just in time, whereas I had to gasp through tryouts during others.

Struggling to watch the countryside whip by at 60 mph, I continue to consider my congestion of yesteryear. I can almost taste those repulsive puffs off inhalers, ever-flowing glasses of OJ, and bottomless bowls of chicken soup. I swear I can smell Vicks VapoRub as my eyelids become heavier and heavier. The rest of the ride home is a blur.

8

February 14

We need to go up one more row," Ron decides. "We can't end on thirteen."

I study the fiber cement siding that my superstitious coworker's crew has installed. Considering the garage was bare when everyone clocked in a few hours earlier, I am impressed with how much progress Ron's team, a trio of green teenagers, has made.

"Not bad," I admit. "Brad would stop there, though. He likes that number."

Ron chuckles, obviously catching my reference to how our boss wrote February 13 two days in a row on next week's calendar.

"Yeah," he smirks. "Brad must have had his heart broken by a girl on Valentine's Day or something."

Yet I don't laugh along with him. I utter nothing, in fact. Instead, I slowly walk away, my steps weighed down by my suddenly heavy heart. Ron has unknowingly struck a chord.

February 14 is a melancholic date for me. It signifies when the world I used to know ended and when my new normal—one I continue to struggle with—began. While most people I know are preoccupied with roses, chocolates, and cards, I remember my dad who, at only 58 years of age, died of pancreatic cancer. I relive the final hours of his life, which ended on Valentine's Day 2011.

It's around 8 PM on the thirteenth when my brother, Jay, enters our father's house for the night shift. He sits down on the opposite side of Pop's bed. I give Dad a hug and I notice he has a profoundly sad expression on his face. We say "I love you" to each other like usual. Prior to leaving the living room, I assure him I'll return in the morning. While I reach for the knob, however, he shouts a phrase I will forever cherish: "I love you, Tyrel!"

I hesitantly close the door behind me. Although my father had always made sure to tell me he loved me, he had never done so in such a loud fashion. I keep replaying this moment in my head as I approach my truck. I get a huge lump in my throat.

I'm home for about an hour, just climbing into bed when Jay calls. He informs me that our pop is in really bad shape. I give my brother the instructions to call the hospice nurse. I let him know Alyssa and I will be there as soon as possible. With great speed, my partner and I get ready. We peel out of the garage. The drive is a blur.

Jay, Alyssa, and I sit beside my dad while he relinquishes this life for the next. He holds on till a little past midnight, peacefully breathing his last at 12:12 AM on February 14. I am convinced he did this on purpose.

On one hand, I believe my father waited until it was officially the fourteenth before he let go because he was a poetic soul. I'm sure he felt that departing while surrounded by those he loved most, not to mention those who loved him most, on the day most associated with love, would be a fitting exit.

On the other hand, I also conclude that Pop wished to leave a powerful impression. During the three decades I had with him, my old man made it quite clear that he thought Valentine's Day was silly, a "Hallmark holiday" to be specific. He believed telling or showing someone love should be expressed unabashedly and with regularity, not solely on February 14. He knew I wholeheartedly shared his philosophy to boot. By passing when he did, Dad actually gave Valentine's Day some meaning.

In truth, those twenty-four hours are now weighty. Despite my refusal to get sucked into the commercialism of the holiday, I pay special attention to Valentine's Day nonetheless. February 14 represents pensiveness, a day to reminisce about my father. This date further prompts me to honor my best friend and the causes he valued most, including end-of-life care.

Hospice provided my pop with some peace, dignity, as well as the privacy and comfort of his own home in his final months. I was grateful for the services he received and wanted to dedicate myself to an effort that had done so much for him. So I became a board member for a local hospice foundation. Rather properly, the first meeting I attended was on February 14, 2012; the one-year anniversary of my dad's death. The most recent gathering occurred on the second anniversary, and I recall the conversation which took place afterwards.

"Happy Valentine's Day, everyone!" Suzanne offers while packing up her belongings.

"Oh, thanks for reminding me!" Fred replies. He suddenly has some pep in his step.

"Last-minute run to the gas station?" I joke. Getting up from the table, I glance at my watch. It's 7:35 PM.

"No, but I do owe my wife a phone call. Have a good night!" Fred disappears down the corridor.

"You too!" I holler.

"Good luck!" adds Suzanne. She then looks over her shoulder at me. "It's a Hallmark holiday if you ask me."

It's a Hallmark holiday…

Standing at the threshold, I ponder those four words. I instantly think of my father. I also muse over four additional words. I flash back to that frigid evening two years ago.

I have no doubt that Pop knew he was going to die soon. That's why he yelled before I walked out. He wanted to make sure the last thing I ever heard from him was "I love you, Tyrel."

My finger on the light switch, I take another gander at the hospice foundation boardroom. I nod with pride. This is my way of saying "I love you, too."

I hesitantly close the door behind me.

9

The Old Man and the GMC

I am looking left, waiting to go right. The traffic of the two-lane highway steadily races by. I lean over the dash. I squint to discern if there are any gaps amongst the leadfooters. The oncoming halogens are rapid and relentless. I recline, resigned to the reality that I'll simply have to be patient until the signal changes. Glancing at the clock, I determine I still have plenty of time to punctually punch in at work. And today has already started better than yesterday. Considering I had to jump my auto twenty-four hours earlier, I can handle the delay.

I try to clean my filthy windshield while in the turn lane. My attempt is futile. Pressing the button merely produces an irritating buzz, and not a single drop of washer fluid. I quickly give up. Figuring my spray nozzles are frozen, I crank the heat to max. The sound of the balmy air blasting via the vents is hypnotic. I study the melting remnants of what I missed with my ice scraper slowly slide down the glass. Then I witness the Ford logo displayed on my horn come to a screeching halt at the very tip of my nose.

WHAM! My ride is slammed forward onto the thoroughfare. By sheer luck I am not crushed, nor do I ram anyone else. Nevertheless, I'm in the worst of places. Not only am I holding up the convoy that wants to move north too, but my truck cab, which is jutting perpendicularly across a lane of rush-hour traffic, is also begging to be broadsided. So I gun it. I complete my hook in fishtail fashion, keep all of my weight on the gas for a half mile, and whip right onto the first available avenue. I immediately pull over. I let my breath out.

Upset yet unscathed, I check out the rearview and pick up on a scarlet pickup (one actually smaller than my Ranger) devoid of its passenger headlight. A gangly, shadowy figure gets out. I do the same.

I step atop the thin layer of fresh snow blanketing the street to meet the elderly guy behind my idling vehicle. He's slightly hunchbacked, bald, sporting Coke-bottle frames, and wearing a beard ZZ Top would endorse.

"Are you alright?" I ask.

He nods. I am annoyed he doesn't echo the question. Shaking my noggin, I point to my busted license plate light.

"Well, this is broken," I say.

"Okay," he finally utters in a hoarse voice.

"This wasn't here." I run my fingers across the softball-sized dent in the lower left portion of my tailgate.

"Okay…"

"And except for these red marks on my bumper, I think that's it."

He's unresponsive. I can tell the wheels are spinning in his mind.

"I thought you were gonna turn back there," he states belatedly.

"What?!"

The senior slaps me on the shoulder. The sky suddenly matches the color of his truck. Glaring back, I do my best to ignore his crooked smile. I practically march through him in order to survey his jalopy.

The old man's early 90s GMC Sonoma is nearing its last legs. The panels are on the verge of falling off the rusty rattletrap, which is not much taller than a picnic table. And its scars are plentiful—dents, scratches, and scrapes of all sizes and shapes riddle the bucket of bolts. Regarding the damage from our collision, the golden-ager confirms what I observed in my rearview as he parked: the passenger side headlamp is bashed out. In fact, the height of the light lines up perfectly with my bumper. It didn't stand a chance the moment gramps rear-ended me.

"Do you have insurance?" I inquire.

"Yeah, but I have to pay to repair this," he replies.

"Can I get your info please?"

"My headlight is gone buddy. You just have to replace a bulb."

"YOU hit ME!"

The old man appears like a deer in his headlights.

"What's your name and phone number?" I continue.

He reluctantly recites his data while I jot it down.

"Listen, I'm the oldest one at the gun shop. If I'm late, they're gonna fire me," he sighs. "So what do ya wanna do?"

I refuse to feel sorry for him because I believe he's trying to gain sympathy. Be that as it may, I don't want to scramble to my job for the second consecutive morning. I don't care to shiver any more than necessary either. I peek over my shoulder. I scan the minor injuries sustained by the weathered truck I've had for a dozen years. The new blemishes are hardly perceptible.

"I'll call you if I need anything," I answer as I pen his plate number.

I don't phone him, though. I conclude it would be much less hassle to live with the dimple and fix the bulb—a cheap, uncomplicated repair—on my own. Still, I'm not entirely free of the old man and the GMC.

A month flies by before I randomly discover the bespectacled fellow, whose headlamps are both intact, pull up next to me at a red. We never make eye contact. Fearful of repeating the past, I cautiously proceed through the green to let the old-timer take the lead. Then he abruptly cuts me off. Braking harshly, I cruise exactly the speed limit till he disappears far up the parkway. I spend the rest of my AM commute wondering if he recognized me or if he's simply an awful motorist in general.

I'm looking right, waiting to go left when I spot the old man coming like a bat out of hell only two weeks later. It's a bright Saturday morn, and he's driving like he hotwired his Sonoma. I allow him to pass prior to entering the frontage road behind him. Despite the few limo lengths between us, I instinctively decelerate. I laugh while he swiftly darts into a residential neighborhood … sans blinker, of course.

Winter becomes spring, and there are no additional sightings of the old man and the GMC. His tin lizzie and reckless maneuvers begin to fade from memory. He is almost forgotten when a reminder strikes me, or rather my Ford, without warning.

I am dragging across the parking lot after a long shift. As I approach my wheels, I notice my driver side taillight is shattered. A closer inspection reveals that the end of my bumper has been pushed in some inches to boot. I sling my backpack into the pickup bed. I throw down my baseball cap in disgust. Sitting on the tailgate, I attempt to cool off before taking on the PM gridlock. I further ponder the identity of the hit-and-runner. I wish the coward would have at least written a note.

I eventually fire up the Ranger. Already consumed by ideas of how to replace my rear lamp, I open the glove compartment. I reach for the owner's guide. Yet my hand stops short of the book. Scribbled on the cover are the old man's name, phone number, and license plate. I shut the glovebox. I decide to web search "taillight installation" once I get home.

10

My Takeaway

The hole in my soul has taken its toll. Nothing, certainly not this tall one I'm nursing, remotely fills the void of losing my dad. I feel isolated in the world, not to mention this dive. I look around. Realizing I'm a forsaken fly at the bar, I blankly stare at the TV high above the spirits. My spirits are low, though. I'm so anxious to be in public that I can't lock eyes with my reflection in the mirror beyond the bottles. I don't have a clue what to do besides sip my brew and pretend to watch the baseball game. I keep peeking left, seeing if a face on the sidewalk belongs to the guy I hesitantly agreed to meet. I return to the screen when somebody slaps me on the back.

"Hey dude," Paul says while occupying the stool on my right.

"Yo," I reply.

"How's life? Everything good?"

"Uh … not really." I'm irritated.

"Who's winning?"

I shrug. "I think the Twins are losing."

The annoying chitchat carries on for several minutes. I am quickly sick of shooting the bull on topics like the humid July weather, beer league softball, and his job despite my joblessness. I start to wonder why Paul requested to hang in the first place. I haven't seen him in six months—prior to my pop's departure—so I assume he wants to know how I'm doing.

It has been bleak since my father died. I'm numb most of the time. I merely drag through the motions from sunup till sundown. My dreadful routine has primarily consisted of tying up the loose ends Dad left behind. He didn't have much in the material sense, hence his debts aren't huge. Still, settling his estate has evoked the emotion I exhibit with regularity: anger. Nobody gives a hoot that Pop passed away; everybody just demands their money. It's been rare to even get an "I'm sorry" on the call. When I explain why it's me phoning and not Jay W. Nelson, the collectors normally respond with silence, a due date, or a few seconds of dead air preceding a deadline. Never before did I figure others could be so heartless. At least I have a buddy like Paul who'll listen. He'll understand.

Nonetheless, he's distracted. He continues squinting past me, more concerned with the activity on the street than his struggling pal of six years. A bell abruptly rings. The glass door swings open.

"There she is!" Paul exclaims.

"Who?" I inquire.

"Stephanie," he answers. "She wanted to meet you."

"Oh…"

"I didn't think you'd mind."

My teeth clench. I squeeze my car keys. I didn't force myself from the safe confines of home for Paul's new girlfriend. I wish he would have told me she'd be stopping by. I assumed Paul and I were going to discuss my father and the hell I've been through after his death. Instead, he is introducing me to his lady. And I'll be damned if I'll talk about my dad with someone I don't know. I wouldn't have agreed to this outing if I had all the details.

Appalled by Paul's disregard, I shut down. He and his speak, I nod, yet I don't hear a word. I can't really remember the rest of my time at the pub except for the color red. What I do recall, however, is that this was the final straw.

In truth, Paul is the latest in a long line of disappointers. Not only have I been met with apathy when handling my pop's affairs, but I've also been utterly dismayed by a lot "friends" since my father succumbed to pancreatic cancer. I vow not to get hurt again. I raise my walls.

During the next eighteen months, I keep people at arm's length. I ignore those who have let me down. Socializing is infrequent at best. I simply talk shop at work. I basically become the neighbor who will communicate across the fence. I'm polite. I can even blab for a bit if the convo remains at the surface. I won't pop over, though. Nor will I invite anyone to do so.

On the other hand, I must escape. The fact I haven't left the country in three years has been gnawing at me. The ghosts of my usual haunts are haunting me to boot. I'm constantly sad because everywhere I glance — the buildings we toiled on together, the parks we visited, the greasy spoons we frequented — reminds me of my old man. So I spend hours upon hours each week searching for ways to flee Minnesota. Unfortunately, my endless Internet surfing doesn't catch a wave which seems right.

I'm soon to write off finding anything. Then, I receive an unexpected email from Alyssa. "What about this?" is the subject. I open her message to discover a forwarded invitation from Habitat for Humanity Guatemala. I read the following sentence: "From April 22 to 26, join us alongside hundreds of national and international volunteers for the construction of 20 homes in Usumatlán, Zacapa, with which we will reach our Casa 50,000."

I am sold. Alyssa knows me extremely well. This trip would satisfy my craving for adventure. In addition, it would bring me back to a place I associate with much happiness, something I haven't felt in forever. Alyssa and I actually met on a Habitat trip to Guatemala. Some of my fondest memories are from the country where we hit it off. It would be nice to return.

Nevertheless, Alyssa can't join me on account of her hectic work and school schedules. And I have grown so reticent that she believes it's probably better for me to travel light. Without her there, I'd have to come out of hiding.

"You have to do this," she insists. "You need to let loose."

I'm in Guatemala two months later. I get acquainted with my fellow volunteers, who are dynamic individuals from all parts and all walks. We put in an exhausting effort in the sweltering lowlands of Zacapa. Assigned to adjacent sites, we help the local masons and families make substantial progress on their houses. Unlike my three previous Habitat trips, however, the build might be the last thing I dwell on.

Entrance to the local cemetery. Usumatlán, Zacapa, Guatemala, April 2013.

What I immediately remember from this experience are the friends I made. I relive the meals, the laughs, the dancing. I shake my head at the nights I should have turned in early for I was fatigued, yet stayed out late because I very much enjoyed my pals' company. I replay the engaging conversations and the wisdom shared with me on our bus rides. I further flash on the moments I opened up about Dad. I still feel the weight floating off my shoulders.

On the eve before I jet, I am given an evaluation to complete. In the survey I am asked for my biggest takeaway from the week. Notwithstanding the rewarding particularities of each excursion, I admit this go-round has especially impacted me.

I realized I am tired of holding my guard up nonstop. I don't aspire to go out a lonely old bird who flew solo his whole life. In Guatemala, the other volunteers displayed their kindness, which, in turn, began to break down my walls. They taught me how to be present again and have fun. Most importantly, they showed me that there are individuals out there who do care.

Pop always said one must change the world through people, but through people I will change my world, too.

Parque Nacional Volcán de Pacaya, Escuintla, Guatemala, April 2013. Photo by Sarah Schneiderwind.

11

Headed for the Devil's Nose

The northbound coach charges into the darkness. Not a word can be heard; the roaring of the motor provides the soundtrack to an otherwise silent ride. Sporadic signs — temporarily visible via the bus's headlights — break up the shadows lining the Pan-American Highway. I squint each moment one of these lonely markers pops up to try to discern how many kilometers remain until Alausí. I only catch postings for destinations like Riobamba, Ambato, and Quito. My anxiety grows. My better half and I departed from Cuenca five hours ago, which according to my travel guide is the approximate time required for this trip. Nevertheless, I've seen jack squat about Alausí, and the *cobrador* (fare collector) hasn't made an announcement. I glance right to check on Alyssa, who is with me in the second row. She is fixed on the opposite roadside. She suddenly leaps from her seat.

"Alausí!" she shouts.

"What?!" I respond. I dart to the front to join her.

"We missed it, Ty!" she exclaims. "The arrow was pointing behind us."

She knocks on the cab door. It swings open, and we are introduced to a cloud of smoke. The cobrador is holding a cigarette between his index and middle fingers.

"Sí," sighs the twentysomething.

"Queremos ir a Alausí," I say. *We want to go to Alausí.*

"Ya pasamos la parada," he replies. *We already passed the stop.*

"Pero pensaba que ustedes iban a pasar por el pueblo," *But I thought you guys were going to pass through town.*

"No," he chuckles. "El pueblo está en el valle. Tienen que tomar un taxi o bajar caminando desde la carretera." *The town is in the valley. You have to take a taxi or walk down from the highway.*

"¡¿Qué hacemos ahora?!" *What do we do now?!*

The vehicle brakes to a complete halt.

"Pueden bajarse aquí," the plump driver suggests. *You can get off here.* A lit cig dangles from his mouth too, rising and falling with his bottom lip when he speaks. "No puedo dar la vuelta," he adds. *I can't turn around.* "La carretera es demasiada estrecha." *The road is too narrow.*

Alyssa and I lock panicky eyes.

"¿Se van a quedar o bajar?" presses the operator. *Are you staying or getting off?*

"La próxima parada está en Riobamba … a poco más de una hora de aquí," the cobrador chimes in. *The next stop is in Riobamba … a little more than an hour away.*

Envisioning the countless wayside shrines I've spotted in Ecuador, I refuse to amble on the shoulder of the Pan-American in the dead of night.

"¡Apúrense!" a patron yells from the rear. *Hurry up!*

"¡Vamos!" someone else screams. *Let's go!*

"Nos bajamos en Riobamba," I answer. *We'll get off in Riobamba.* I glare toward the back upon return to our seats.

Alausí Canton, Chimborazo Province, Ecuador, May 2014

Alyssa curls beneath her fleece jacket. She shuts her lids. My peepers, on the other hand, are wide open. Interlacing my fingers to the webbing, I rest my elbows on my knees. I concentrate on the floor. I do my best to ignore the laughter coming from the cab. After an eternity, the coach gradually decelerates. The cobrador pokes his head out.

"¡Riobamba!" he shouts.

Following Alyssa, I give the collector fare for two. He thanks me. I proceed without uttering a word.

We step into dreariness. A handful of taxis creep back and forth along the dim avenue. I don't signal one, however, because I have no idea where to go. The only further indications of life come from a smattering of people eating at a nearby food cart. We approach.

"¿Dónde hay un buen hotel?" I inquire. *Where is a good hotel?*

"La Quinta Macají," a middle-aged cowboy responds without hesitation.

"¿La Quinta Macají?" I repeat for confirmation.

"Sí, es muy buena." *Yes, it is very nice.*

I thank the dude and promptly hail an oncoming sedan. Climbing into the auto, I note that the driver briefly pauses when I tell him to bring us to La Quinta Macají. I figure he needs a sec to process my accent.

The vehicle veers onto a forlorn boulevard five minutes later. Steering south on Avenida 9 de Octubre, the cabbie abruptly parks in front of a tall white wall. The enclosure lines the parkway for a couple of blocks.

"La Quinta Macají," he affirms, pointing to the bleached barricade at our three.

Understanding *quinta* to be "country home" in Spanish, I hop out expecting to locate the gate to a fancy villa.

"¿Dónde está la entrada?" I probe. *Where's the entrance?*

"Allí," the leadfoot replies. He nods to a driveway at the end of the pavement.

The car races off. Alyssa and I make for the corner. We sadly encounter more obscurity beyond the bend—no sound, no lights, not a soul in sight. We are in an alley. Revisiting the main road, I scan the barrier. I spot a wooden sign which reads, "La Quinta Macají." The name is correct, yet my idea of *quinta*, in this case, is wrong. I realize we are frowning at the wall of a large farm.

Pissed off for being duped, I yank my guidebook out of my bag. I frantically flip the pages till I arrive at accommodations in Riobamba. While I skim the section, my partner alertly flags a taxi she sees on the other side of the divided highway. It hangs a U-ey at the next intersection.

"¿Cuál es el mejor hotel en Riobamba?" I pry through the passenger window. *What is the best hotel in Riobamba?*

"Hotel Zeus," the young man answers.

Recognizing the name from my speed-read, I let my breath out. I follow Alyssa into the rear of the compact.

A left and a right—separated by a stint on Duchicela—lead us to the steps of Hotel Zeus. Alyssa and I check in, drop our bags in our room, and instantly retrace our steps to the lobby. We exit the building in desperate search of dinner. We plod atop Avenida Daniel León Borja for a stretch in each direction, but fail to locate an open establishment. Alyssa reads her watch. It's almost eleven o'clock.

"It's Thursday night," she states. "Everything probably closes at ten."

At the hotel once again, we ask the clerk if the restaurant is open. He must sense we are hungry because, even though there are no additional employees to be seen, he tells us to have a seat. He trails us to our table.

"¿Les puedo ofrecer un sándwich?" he offers. *Can I make you a sandwich?*

We eagerly nod. The young server, who is doubling as our cook, disappears beyond the swinging kitchen door. He soon reappears with our food. We inhale the sandwiches.

"That's the best grilled cheese I've ever had," my lady admits with a smile. I agree.

Grateful for his kindness, we discuss how the guy could have simply told us the restaurant was closed. We leave a nice tip on the table. We go to the reception to thank him before taking the elevator to our suite before collapsing on our bed.

I wake up to hear Riobamba's Friday is well underway. I open the curtains to pastel structures illuminated by a brilliant dawn. A cacophony of cars honking, dogs barking, and roosters crowing fills the air. Flea-like pedestrians scurry about the sidewalks. Among the hustle and bustle, I notice buses rolling in and out of the Terminal Terrestre. It is merely four blocks to the west; an easy commute for a change.

We arrive at the depot an hour later. Entering the lot, we immediately identify "Alausí" painted across a red and white bus, which is beginning to pull out of its parking space. We run to the coach and jump on. We plop ourselves behind the operator. I grab my book. We study up on the Nariz del Diablo (Devil's Nose) train ride. We can hardly keep still for the ensuing hundred kilometers.

Our transportation exits the Pan-American Highway just past 10 AM. Slowly descending into Alausí, I observe the striking pueblo; the cute, colorful buildings remind me of a LEGO town. Alyssa and I disembark in the center of the community. We drag along the main drag, 5 de Junio, until we reach the tiny plaza at the end. Back of the square sits the train station. We get to the ticket counter with fifteen minutes to spare. (Check-in closing is 10:30, a half hour prior to departure.)

Fifty bucks lighter, I slip Alyssa her *billete de tren*. I follow her to the cement platform beyond the depot. We join a camera-flashing crowd of roughly thirty people, varying in age and nationality. At half past ten the train comes into the terminal, and the early risers who caught the 8 AM hop off. I examine the vintage carriages as we wait for permission to board. Despite their old-fashioned appearance, the timbered wagons shine new, like someone has recently applied wood polish. My number one and I eventually enter car 1566. Ten fellow travelers grab chairs around us. The charcoal locomotive starts southward at eleven o'clock on the dot.

A young host stands with a microphone. He first speaks in English, then Spanish. He describes the history of the railroad in the region while the train snakes over creeks, below trees, and between rolling green hills. The hills gradually grow into grassy mountains. And

San Pedro de Alausí, Chimborazo, Ecuador, May 2014

Alausí Canton, Chimborazo Province, Ecuador, May 2014

the cliffs to our left occasionally inch so close that a daring individual could actually touch the jags by opening a window. In the meantime, the view to our right subsequently transforms into a sharp drop-off. Peering into the bottom of the gorge, I notice a red-roofed structure positioned amid two trackways. I determine it must be the Sibambe Station when the train begins its unique descent. I realize we are on the Devil's Nose.

Made possible with a couple of switchbacks, the train zigzags down the steep mount. It starts head first. Passing a convergence in the tracks, it then reverses down the second stretch of rails before completing the zigzag in a forward motion. At the foot of the peak, the engine chugs to a viewpoint well past the Sibambe Station. Everyone detrains to witness the Devil's Nose from afar. Alyssa and I meander about the gravelly lookout with the other sightseers for a bit. We take pictures and take in the famous Nariz del Diablo.

"¿De dónde viene el nombre?" I ask our guide, who is posing as a photographer for most of the spectators. *Where does the name come from?*

He gives me two potential origins. I disagree with his first statement that the mountain resembles a face with a giant snout. I nonetheless find his second reason much more believable. Though the great feat in engineering of the switchbacks was ultimately accomplished, he says the bluff is dubbed "Devil's Nose" for the countless rail construction fatalities that occurred between Sibambe and Alausí.

Alyssa and I reenter the wagon. The locomotive barely gets moving prior to halting next to the Sibambe depot at noon. Tourists and crew alike shuffle into the cement block building for lunch. After wolfing our complimentary sandwiches, my partner and I ascend a long staircase to the Cóndor Puñuna (Condor Nest) visitor center, which overlooks the terminus from an adjacent ledge. Alyssa ventures inside. I stay outside to absorb the cloudy, yet tranquil scenery. Leaning on the safety railing, I survey the lush valley. I study the brook swerving through the canyon. I beam at the stream till it curves behind a distant cliff. An arm wraps around my shoulders.

"There's going to be a dance performance in a few minutes," Alyssa reveals. "We should get down there."

We quickly sit on the edge of the tiny souvenir plaza near the base of the steps. Five men and five women, who are dressed in traditional Andean attire, own the concrete stage. The males don white shirts and pants, red shawls, black shoes, and cream hats. The women have similar hats, but sport red skirts with their black flats, white blouses, and off-white shawls. Pan flutes playfully pipe. Each holding a different colored streamer, the performers dance in a loop, twisting the ribbons around a tall wooden pole in the middle of their circle. The women do the second song themselves. They fold, stretch, and fling their shawls for the entire number. When the music ends, so does our time at the Devil's Nose.

It's 1:30 when we arrive back in Alausí. Ready to return to Cuenca, Alyssa and I hit Main Street until we reach the terminal. We walk up to a man who is leaning against the depot with arms crossed.

"¿Dónde cogemos el autobús para Cuenca?" I inquire. *Where do we catch the bus for Cuenca?*

Nariz del Diablo, Sibambe, Alausí, Ecuador, May 2014. Photo by Alyssa Nelson.

"En la carretera," he acknowledges. *On the highway.*

I shift my gaze up to the distant Pan-American. My shoulders slump.

"Mi carro está ahí," he continues, nodding toward a taxi on my left. *My car is right there.* "Los llevo por un dólar." *I'll drive you for a dollar.*

Alyssa and I jump into the yellow coupe. In a wink, the cabbie burns rubber down 5 de Junio and spins his wheels up the hill. He swiftly pulls into a gas station.

"¿Esperamos aquí?" I dig while digging some coins out of my pocket. *We wait here?*

He nods. "No tendrán que esperar mucho." *You won't have to wait long.*

We get out, and the speedster whips a U-turn. He descends the hill faster than he climbed it.

"Do you believe him?" questions my companion. "This is kind of sketchy."

I watch the winding *Panamericana* as far as my eyes take me in each direction. I see no autos whatsoever.

"Yeah, hopefully a bus comes soon," I reply.

Yet I'm not worried. We missed this stop less than sixteen hours ago, which led us to being misled and lost on a gloomy street in Riobamba. We found a way to the Devil's Nose anyhow. We are a tenacious team. No matter the twist, I know we will get to Cuenca somehow.

We head for the shoulder in front of the gas pumps. We shortly pick up the sound of an engine to the north. It's getting louder and louder. We stand. A coach suddenly barrels around the mountain. Alyssa, whose vision is clearly better than mine, focuses on the sign in the approaching windshield. I grin when she sticks her pointer finger in the air.

12

Roughing it (in)

It is common for tradesmen in Minnesota to "rough in" or "dry in" new homes prior to the arrival of winter. To "rough in" a dwelling means to build its foundation and frame, staple housewrap to the walls, mount the windows and exterior doors, and complete the roof. Contractors prefer to reach this point ahead of the chill so they'll have protection from the elements while they carry on with the interior. The same concept applies to garages. Though there are fewer tasks, carpenters would rather stand panels in T-shirts instead of thermals, for every duty is easier in milder weather. For example, it is much less taxing to pound support posts into the ground when it isn't frozen solid.

Unfortunately, Jack Frost had beaten my YouthBuilders and me—the Tree Trust Lead Construction Trainer—to site by the time we were to start a garage in North Minneapolis. It was a fortnight before Christmas, and my crew of powerhouses hadn't a clue how to break the ice. Our lumber was blanketed in several inches of white powder; far too late to put up a "dry box." We'd rarely be dry, let alone warm, in the next four months.

But shivering wasn't the only obstacle my team of nine teens and I would have to surmount. We spent many mornings shoveling. We then salted the paths we cleared in order to unload equipment from the truck and subsequently arrange workstations. On most of these occasions, we were already clocked in for an hour till we got going. Moreover, the north edge of the structure was merely a few feet from the bordering garage and property fence. So it was nearly impossible to avoid bumping a tool, ladder, or limb into the neighbor's carport or chain link. This slender stretch could be an icy shower to boot. Because there was no room to move, those drudging under the north eve while the temp was north of freezing would be rained on with melting snow runoff. The YBers duly deemed this area the "bad side." Toiling above proved problematic as well. In fact, a pair of low-hanging electrical lines almost touched the roof. We, therefore, had to wait patiently for the power company to cut the current to proceed with the cap.

Regardless of the difficulties, my squad was never dissuaded. After pounding rebar stakes (since the wooden ones quickly splintered) into the frozen earth, the gamers stood and braced the perimeter by December 20. They had the roof trusses set in January. Covering the crown with plywood shortly afterwards, the fireballs also plastic-wrapped three of the walls by February's end. The aluminum soffit and fascia were done on Saint Patrick's Day. The hot shots then finished the siding for the south façade on March 20. And they nailed in the final shingle on Tax Day.

Ross (left) and me, Minneapolis, Minnesota, June 2014. Photo by Jennie Uttech.

"Open Campus Day" occurred on April 17. Various Tree Trust staff and a couple of parents visited the jobsite to view what the program participants had accomplished. In spite of the countless compliments they received, I noticed how often the achievers brought up the ensuing boxes to check on the vacant home occupying the lot. They wished to see the project, one that had tested them each step of the way, through to the very end … even if the upcoming trials were to escalate. I relive one uphill battle in particular.

The shingles are closer to banana peels. The mid-June sun bakes our napes while Ross Dale and I fight to stay upright on a slope doing its best to fling us off. The steep pitch practically shoves our steel-toes into our shins. My ankles ache. My calves kill. Waiting for the new window to appear via the rough opening, Ross and I observe the steady flow of sweat droplets splattering on our boots. The humidity combined with the weight of our fall protection and tool belts is causing rather productive perspiration.

"I'm dying up here," the high-flyer says. He wipes his brow with the back of his hand.

"I hear ya," I reply. "Let's put this one in and then we can take off these harnesses."

"We won't need them anymore?"

"Nope. We can do the last four from ladders."

Ross grins. He grabs for the glass, which is brought to us by a pair of his peers laboring within the gutted duplex.

All flanges of the window are nailed and flashed fifteen minutes later. I ask one of the indoor helpers to secure a ladder to the edge of the eve. I tell Ross to shake a leg. Unsure of how to reach the rungs, he places both palms on the shingles. Crawling on all fours—feet first—is the approach he chooses. Yet he remains stuck in downward dog. My impatience resurfaces.

"What the heck are you doing?!"

"This is sketchy."

"Ross, stand up."

"I can't!"

"Lower yourself like I taught you." Backing down slowly as I adjust my slack, I demonstrate the technique. "Stay calm; you've done this a bunch."

"It's loose!" He anxiously feeds his rope forward through the grab.

"Because you're creating more slack!" I quickly climb to him. "Tighten your line and trust your gear."

"I don't know, man."

"I made sure our rigging was safe," I affirm. "I don't wanna fall either."

Ross laughs. He carefully straightens up and warily descends to the ladder. I follow.

"You panicked up there." I unbuckle my chest clip.

"Yeah," Ross acknowledges while shaking his head. "Heights are still kind of hard for me."

"It will become easier … if you keep trying."

"I'll get there."

He kept his word. In truth, Ross was tied to a peak for the entire next week. By Friday afternoon, he was a natural in his harness. I wasn't surprised; he was simply displaying the tenacity required to succeed on a YB program.

Ross and his teammates were some of the most determined students I had ever worked with. Notwithstanding their admission of wanting to walk off the frigid turf at some point, they grinded thirty hours every other week, and eventually conquered the coldest winter of their lives. The group additionally maintained excellent attendance at their respective high schools from October until their YouthBuild graduation in May.

Confronting fears, pressing on, and learning how to balance a lot of responsibility are major reasons why these go-getters continue to thrive. Ross recently landed a position with a local landscaping company. And his friends on the Advanced Summer Crew keep knocking out complicated projects, such as staircases, exterior doors, and a roof remodel. But that's just talking shop.

After watching these dynamos grow into their own during the past ten months, I have the utmost confidence in them, jobsite or not. They are skilled. They are reliable. They are undaunted. Whether they are facing a fresh challenge, taking on extra commitments, or pursuing their goals, I expect them to come out on top. I know they'll get there.

13

A Comfortable Silence

We haven't seen each other in four years. We have spoken occasionally — guilty calls on birthdays and holidays — but we haven't actually been face-to-face since the spring after my pop died. That's what happens when two extremely stubborn people disagree. Nevertheless, a random, yet serious phone call from my mother had me at her porch on this May day. I open the weathered screen. I rap loudly on the door.

"Come in!"

I take a deep breath, take a step forward, and am instantly taken aback. Although she's naturally small (five feet on her tiptoes), I notice a notably gaunter version of the Filipina I had in my mind. She lifts her scrawny right arm to run a comb through her thick, jet-black hair. The type 2 diabetes has done a number on her; she can't be more than a hundred pounds soaking wet.

"You look good," she remarks with a wide smile.

"So do you," I muster despite the lump in my throat.

"You ready?"

I nod. She throws on a leather baseball cap. She reaches for her jacket, and I raise my brows for it is sunny and seventy outside. She locks her trailer and trails me to my pickup.

"Do you need help getting in?" I ask, opening the Ranger.

"No, I got it."

She clenches the "oh shit" bar and swiftly climbs in. Surprised by her nimbleness, I shut the door for her.

"Thank you, Son," she says upon rolling down her window.

For the next twenty minutes, I am distracted by her constant fidgeting. If she's not running her fingernails across her shins, she's rasping her forearms or the nape of her neck.

She's grimacing. I begin to worry.

"Are you okay, Mom? Why do you keep scratching yourself?"

"The diabetes makes me itch all over," she answers with a sigh. "My doctor says it's from bad circulation."

She updates me on her failing kidneys, the unending appointments at the clinic, and the many medications she's on. She abruptly pauses every so often to shout last-second directions. I nonetheless remain quiet. Due to her poor health, she's hardly driven for several years, which has kept her home most of the time. Aware her opportunities to vent are rare, I simply listen, doing my best to lend her an ear. She rattles off umpteen unpronounceable pills while I veer into the parking lot of her credit union.

Gleaming, she stares through the windshield.

"I've been coming to this place forever," she beams. "Everyone knows me here."

My mom and I are soon seated at a table around the corner from the tellers' counter. A pair of women—one with dark hair, the other with light—approach us.

"Hi Elizabeth!" the brunette exclaims. "We heard you need a couple of witnesses."

"Yes."

"So what are we signing here, Ms. Nelson?" the blonde inquires. She squints at the documents on the table.

My mother looks to me.

"Her health care directive and last will and testament," I respond.

There's an uncomfortable silence. I imagine the ladies' deer-in-headlights expression to be like mine at Mom's front door earlier.

"This is Tyrel, my oldest," my mom states, breaking up the awkwardness.

"You go first," I prompt my mother. I point to her papers.

She initials. She signs. They sign. She initials. She signs. They sign.

"He's a writer," Mom proudly continues. "He's traveled all over Latin America."

I feel my mug getting warm.

"I call him Peregrine because he's always flying somewhere," my mom reveals.

Both women chuckle.

"And he knew how to get these forms done," she goes on. She brings the will to her grill. She narrows her peepers to study the fresh autographs. "He's a good son."

My eyes well up. I shift them to the floor, desperately trying to hide the drops that are forming. I quickly use my sleeves to wipe off my tears. I refocus on the ladies to thank them for their help. My mother thanks them to boot, referring to each as "Dear." I gather the documents, and we make for the exit.

"Bye, Elizabeth!" yells a young teller. He is in the middle of helping a customer.

"Bye-bye, Ryan!"

Back in the Ford, a tiny hand grabs my right wrist when I'm about to turn the key.

"Thank you for doing this, Son."

"Of course," I assert. "I helped Dad with his will, so I kind of knew what to do already."

"How much do I owe you?"

"Don't worry about it," I urge. "Jay's going to split the cost with me."

"This is a big weight off my shoulders," Mom confesses. "I want to stay around for you guys, but just in case I…"

"I know," I interrupt. "You're not done, though. You still have things to do."

"Yeah, like hold a grandchild!" She wisecracks. "You and Alyssa should have at least two, hopefully one of each."

"I'll see what I can do," I reply with a smirk. I fire up the engine.

Pulling up to her single-wide, my mom requests I check out her garden. I oblige. I am not surprised by what's in front of me. In fact, the plot resembles many she's tended throughout my life. Her flowers are bright and plentiful. The plants are thick and thriving. Everything is green as can be, including her thumb.

I spend the ensuing hour shadowing the Filipina across her flourishing yard. She presents the tulips my bro planted last spring, not to mention the stout bird bath a friend gave her. She proceeds to show me numerous impressions left by her border rocks, which were swiped by crooks clearly lacking stones. She further informs me of her goal to squirrel away as much of the little dough she receives from the government before visiting family in the Philippines next winter. She brings up the trip when Jay and I accompanied her to her homeland nearly fifteen years ago.

"I wish your father would have gone with us," she admits. "He could have given you and your brother a tour of Subic Bay, where he was stationed."

"Yeah, that would've been neat," I agree.

"You know I talk to him, Son?"

In spite of their divorce while I was a kid, my parents still cared for one another. I was in the room when Pop uttered "I love you, Beth" from his hospice bed. I infer from my mother's puppy-dog frown that his death continues to bore a hole in her soul.

"That's great," I affirm. "I talk to him almost every day."

She sticks her arms out. I give her a big hug.

"Well, I should get going," I suggest.

"You have the same lines around your eyes as me," she acknowledges.

"I also have your flat nose," I add.

We share a long laugh.

"I love you, Mom."

"I love you too, Son."

I hop in my truck, roll down the window, and turn to her. She's grinning. So am I. There's a comfortable silence.

On the highway home, I reflect on the up-and-down relationship my mom and I have had. I ponder the peaks, and all the time I've lost with her during the valleys, especially this latest ebb. I think of her frail condition, which drives me to put our differences in the rearview. And I replay the afternoon we've just spent together, which makes me realize how much I have missed her.

Mom's gardens, Blaine, Minnesota, May 2015

14

Guatemala Revealed

A blaring buzzer abruptly invades my dreams. I have fallen from that castle in the air to land on the bed of my shadowy hotel room. My eyes are wide open, but I can't see a thing. I frantically fumble for my phone atop the nightstand. I finally manage to swipe off the alarm, yet my ears are still ringing—most likely a residual effect from the rock music that filled the streets of Antigua until the wee hours.

I hurry through a shower. I notice that dawn is forcing itself around the curtains when I exit the bathroom. Soon there's a knock at the door.

"¿Señor Nelson?" a woman asks from the hallway.

"Sí."

"El conductor lo espera." *The driver is waiting for you.*

"Ya voy." *I am on my way.*

I shove the last of my possessions into my suitcase before yanking the zipper to the end of its line. Catching up to the receptionist, I hand over my key just as she returns to the front desk. My journey back to Minneapolis has begun.

I am slouched in a seat in Guatemala City a little over an hour later. I look up from my Android to notice a lady with a tablet approaching me in the terminal. Conducting a survey, she wonders if I'd be willing to share with her what I like most about the country.

Having been to Guatemala a few times, I don't know where to start. But my senses come alive. I picture the picturesque panoramas of Lake Atitlán, and the colorful villages scattered along its mountainous shores. I hear the high school bands parading through the streets of La Estancia on a sunny afternoon. I feel the splinters from inspecting a handmade door in a tiny shop tucked away in the highlands. I detect a hint of sulfur that continues to check in with me while hiking Volcán Pacaya. And I taste the zesty *jocotes* given to me in the lowlands of Usumatlán.

Be that as it may, I reflect on the individuals tied to these experiences more than anything. The pulpy jocotes take me to a sweltering day of homebuilding in the department of Zacapa. I vividly remember Daisy, the future owner of the residence, tapping me on the shoulder. The offering of red fruit was her way of turning me away from the work for a much-needed breather. The trail on the volcano leads me to Juan, the kind man who led our group up and down Pacaya. Not only did I get to know him, but I also got to meet his brother José, who we ran into while he guided other trekkers. The slivers from the carpentry stir up a conversation with a local woodworker southeast of Xela. I nearly chuckle upon recalling some of the jokes we exchanged. The procession in La Estancia jogs my memory about the grocery runs I did with Nicolasa and Evelina to the town's market. Their home cooking kept our crew of volunteers well fed for a week and a half. Lastly, the amazing views direct me to the drivers, such as Eladio, who drove my teammates and me across beautiful landscapes, stopping at scenic overlooks along the way. It was Eladio, in fact, who was parked on the cobblestones outside of Casa Rustica this morning. Because he had picked me up from the airport a couple weeks earlier, I instantly recognized his moustache-capped smile when I stepped out of the inn. He told me all about his wife, kids, not to mention his pet turtle, before dropping me off at La Aurora International.

"¿Qué es lo que más le gusta de Guatemala?" the woman inquires. *What do you like most about Guatemala?*

"La gente," I reply. *The people.*

Cantel, Quetzaltenango, Guatemala, July 2015

15

From 36 to 63

One of the first things I did after turning 36 was pull a hamstring. In an attempt to prove to myself and my softball teammates that I hadn't lost a step, I tried to shift into a higher gear while rounding the bases. I ended up a peg leg instead.

Sixteen days later, I am pacing back and forth in a park reserve. The sun on this Saturday morn shines bright. The fall colors are on the verge of peaking. My T-shirt and wind pants are the perfect attire on this 19th day of September. Many would say the conditions are ideal for a 5k, yet I am concerned. I never train very seriously for road races—a few neighborhood laps staggered between hot yoga sessions at most. I wasn't able to do much apart from short walks aided by a brace. So my endurance isn't where I'd like it to be. And although my hammy has improved significantly since I limped off the diamond, it remains quite tight.

Then again, I won't be stopped. Not only is this event to raise money and awareness for pancreatic cancer, but the 5k is a way to honor survivors and those who have died from the disease as well. I have to do this for Dad, who departed four and a half years ago.

I try to do some last-minute stretches. The crowd thickens. I reach for my toes and arrive nowhere close. I stand up to notice Alyssa's smirk. She puts her forearm on my shoulder. She stretches her quad.

"Will the faster people please come to the front?" a Mike with a mic requests.

"Are you ready?" Alyssa asks.

"I guess we'll see," I sigh.

"You're gonna do great," she encourages. "You should get up there."

I take a deep breath. I give her a kiss and make for the starting line.

"Open it up, Nelson!" Alyssa shouts.

The announcer's countdown hits zero. I begin at an average speed. The ultra-tight wrap on my hamstring seems to be working, so I pick up the pace about a quarter mile in. I glide by several participants. I fall in behind the handful of leaders. I fear that sharp twinge I had in my left leg a fortnight back, so I stay at three-quarter speed, which is fast enough to pass a couple more.

I am in fourth place by the first marker. My adrenaline is flowing, and I feel like I can run forever. My breathing is steady, my strides quick and light. I hit the hills of the winding route at nearly full tilt. Cruising by another person, I key on the guy in second. He approaches a tiny table (the midpoint), which is an odd sight in the center of this vast woodland. He swipes a cup from the young man manning the station.

Roughly thirty ticks later, I reach the volunteer. The flyer ahead of me took water, so I figure it couldn't hurt. I slow down to grab some. But I am not used to drinking and dashing. I struggle to swallow half the cup; the rest splashes on my face. The water grossly swishes in my stomach. I immediately become sluggish.

I am in a bad place by the next marker. My perspiration is flowing, and I feel like I haven't run in forever. My breathing is heavy, and the silver sprinter is nowhere in sight. Detecting distant footsteps, I glance past my shoulder to spot the dude I just passed. He's gaining, and if I continue this nosedive, he'll soon leapfrog me. My competitiveness takes control. I get mad. I promise myself that, no matter what, I will not be caught.

Staring at the trail, I manage to recapture momentum. My mind wanders off course, though. Gasping and heart pounding provide the soundtrack to a reel of my father. Scrolling down memory lane, I recall how he always gave his best—I imagine him telling me to do the same in this race. I further remember him sick in bed, telling me how he wished he could help me with the household chores. Then I think of those currently stricken with cancer and how they'd probably give anything to simply jog again. A burst of speed comes on.

Third is still mine by the third marker. A girl who is standing at the sign claps loudly.

"You're almost there!" she cheers.

I open it up. All I hear is wheezing during the final tenth of a mile. Tears form. All I see is a distant balloon arch jolting up and down with my stomps. A yellow tent develops in the corner of my eye. I focus on the vertical "FINISH" banner next to the canopy. I can practically touch it! I lunge.

"Nice push!" an onlooker screams.

Stumbling for a spell, I ultimately find my balance. I plod beyond the finish line with my hands behind my noggin, sucking as much wind as possible. A lady suddenly appears.

"You placed third overall," she states. "Congratulations!"

She gives me a bronze medal. A faint "thank you" is what I can muster. We pose for a picture. The lady suddenly disappears.

Gladly wearing my prize around my neck, I stand to the side of the archway to wait for Alyssa. I recognize her easy strides after a bit. I anticipate the explosion.

"C'mon Alyssa!" I yell.

She opens it up. Her smooth gait grows into a gallop. Her eyes burn holes through those in front of her. She fiercely pumps her arms. She looks powerful, twice as fast as the small group she passes. She crosses the line with a full head of steam. I meet her when her wheels stop spinning.

"Way to go!" I exclaim while giving Alyssa a high five.

"You too," she replies, nodding toward my award. "I knew you could do it!"

I wake up relieved the following morning. Notwithstanding the tightness in my hammy, there is no additional pain. I mosey to the couch. I sip my coffee in comfortable silence. Reflecting on yesterday, I eventually get up to fetch my hardware.

I lift the medal off my dad's picture frame. I turn it over and over again. A strange mix of satisfaction and sadness hits me. Pop would have been proud.

He would have also been 63 today.

16

Looking Back on White Earth

My father saw gnomes as he neared death. They started with their backs against the paneled walls of his living room, moving closer and closer to him each day. He wasn't scared, though. Rather, he appeared to be comforted by them. After Dad died, a hospice grief counselor told me that it isn't rare for people to observe things — humans, hounds, hobbits all the same — shortly before they are to breathe their last. Not only do the figures circle in, but they also take the shape of something familiar, lightening to the dying while they prepare for departure. I smiled upon hearing this. Pop was a Tolkien fan, so it was fitting that trolls ushered him into the next life. I got goosebumps to boot.

Several years pass until I get such shivers again. It's late in the evening in the middle of May. Nine students from Carroll University, their professor, and I are hunkered on the edge of the White Earth Powwow Grounds in northwestern Minnesota. Dressed in layers and huddled beneath blankets, we strain our eyes to decipher the shadowy shapes in front of us. The trajectories of our visible breaths lead us to dim flashlight beams. We trace the rays back to tiny clusters of silhouettes seated amongst the metallic bleachers of the sanctified arena. A light fog has crept in from the adjacent forest to join in attendance. An almost full moon softly glows over a faint white structure at the bullseye of the revered ring. The construction has the form of a circular shower curtain, and the ends of branches are jutting out of the top. Suddenly, a handful of men sitting next to the tent beat their drums and belt out loudly. The singing eventually tapers off, and the reverberations echo into the distance.

Every so often, a drummer leaves the center to escort individuals from one of the patient groups back to the tent. Those who are taken to the tent kneel before a small gap at the bottom. The kneelers articulate their names, where they are from, and present a cloth that identifies their tribe. They then ask for advice concerning a specific problem (e.g., health) with which they are struggling. The tent shakes in response to each petition, sometimes quite vigorously. When the quavering stops, counsel is contributed from inside the tent. Requests carry on through the night. We watch until the cold air ultimately grows unbearable.

The following morning our Anishinaabe (uh-nish-ih-nah-bay) guide, a well-respected local sage, fields the various questions we have about the ceremony. He reveals that the tent shakes upon contact with the spirits. The higher beings, in turn, yield the helpful information which is sought. Although he cannot clarify what exactly happens inside, he asserts that the advice imparted the previous night did not come from a person.

Two days after the shaking tent, the Carroll crew and I return to the hallowed site with dozens of cedar seedlings. The Anishinaabe have long cherished cedar. Moreover, they utilize it to protect rarified locations and timberlands. Given that a forest provides the backdrop to the White Earth Powwow Grounds, it is understandable that our volunteer team has been asked to add more cedar trees to this numinous neck of the woods.

We spend the duration of that dewy dawn planting all over the area. We visit other establishments important to the community, such as the White Earth Reservation Tribal DOVE (Down on Violence Everyday) women's shelter, Indian Health Clinic, White Earth Senior Apartments, and White Earth Tribal Headquarters. We root the remainder of our three hundred seedlings at a K-12 institute. We are invited inside for a midday snack.

A dynamic voice abruptly bursts through the double doors a few minutes later. The cacophony of convo, chuckles, and clanging silverware no longer occupies the lunchroom. Returning our PB and J and tiny milk cartons to their respective slots on our plastic trays, we give our undivided attention to a middle-aged fellow sporting a ponytail. He strides to a long table, putting one of his feet atop its bench. He rests his forearms on his bent knee. He leans in.

The speaker has a captivating presence. Even though he addresses the entire squad, he locks eyes with everyone, making it seem like he's communicating with us individually. The man goes on to thank us for all the hard work we've done to find homes for the baby conifers around Circle of Life Academy. The principal is principally contented with our efforts because cedar on the White Earth Reservation has become scarce. He further explains that cedar is sacred, sacred locally due to its ceremonial, religious, and medicinal purposes. As a small token of his appreciation, he subsequently lays out the steps for how to draw on the trees we've been planting for a common ailment. He concludes his expression of gratitude by affirming that, albeit intangible, his gift—a bestowal of knowledge—is one which can last forever, especially since it can be passed down to others.

Not only do the Anishinaabe continue to heed the wisdom of their ancestors, generations upon generations have also used drums in their ceremonies. During our final evening on White Earth, the Carroll group and I are invited to a drum ceremony. We are simply encouraged to bring food and to dress respectfully. When receiving this offer, my mind immediately skips to booming beats—thunderous rolls coming from Native drummers who erupt into song. Yet no tunes can be heard while we pull up to the peaceful pond. And drums are not struck under the roof of the small lakeside cabin either. Instead, we strike a buffet.

Donating our big pot of taco soup to a large spread of chili, hot dogs, chicken, and bologna sandwiches, we soon discover that the intention of this gathering was not about percussion but recognition. The homeowner states that he is holding this ceremonial dinner to honor his powwow drum, which is proudly displayed behind him in the dining room. He earnestly speaks of his connectedness to the instrument, referring to a kindred soul, a loyal companion instead of solely an object to produce music. He, his brother, and a couple of women from the community openly answer our inquiries about this custom and other Anishinaabe traditions. They also disclose deep stories about themselves. Similarly, they ask questions to get to know our crew better. The sincerity they've displayed makes us comfortable in delivering from the heart, too. Honesty is fully shown. Ardent accounts are shared. Even some tears are shed. We convey our indebtedness to our newfound friends for inviting us to such a personal, powerful event. The owner says we are always welcome in his home.

In the handshake line leading to the door, we repeatedly tell our hosts that we don't want to leave the reservation. We take some last pictures together on the shore behind the house prior to hitting the road. The scenery is postcardlike. Laconism lulls the lakefront. Time stands still. The fading sun, shoreline evergreens, and glassy water are the perfect background to a mesmerizing experience on White Earth.

Naytahwaush, Mahnomen County, White Earth Reservation, Minnesota, May 2017

In truth, part of me remains at my dad's bedside, hearing him matter-of-factly describe the gnomes nearby. I can still see the tent shaking on those twilit powwow grounds. I continue to feel the true weight of the cedar in my hands. And I keep striving to drum up moments as senseful as those in that place on reflective pond.

Without a doubt, I find these occasions to be incredibly humbling and meaningful. Humbling in that I was allowed into such profound windows. Meaningful due to their authenticity—unique occurrences viewed in their purest form.

My pop once remarked that "all things are beautiful when honestly displayed." I can honestly say that beauty is on full display on White Earth.

17

Seven Hours

It's difficult for me to say this, but final team meeting adjourned!" I exclaim.

Smiles fill the lunchroom. Applause echoes down the corridors of the community center. While we clap in unison, I beam with pride at the ten Carroll Pioneers. For a week the seven ladies and three gents plodded through planting projects across the White Earth Reservation. And the expressions on their faces show me that they, too, are satisfied with the mark they have left on northwestern Minnesota.

Despite a four-hour drive to Minneapolis in the morning, I stay up because it's my last eve with the college group. I lose to the girls repeatedly in basketball. I lose to a future Navy SEAL in a race. I manage to win a couple games of pool. Eventually bidding everyone goodnight, I inch to the locker room. May 19 becomes May 20. Weak from a week of being on twenty-four seven, I virtually snooze below the showerhead.

Nevertheless, I have to lock the game room prior to hitting my sleep sack. Returning to the commissary for my keys, I go to the adjacent storage room. Yet after trying the handle, I'm not sure if I can handle what I think has just happened—not this late anyhow. In disbelief, I give it another shot. Oh no. I set my toiletry bag and towel on a nearby table. Grasping the knob tightly, I tug as hard as I can, but it's to no avail. I turn around. I put my hands atop my crown. My bloodshot eyes stare into the dimly lit dining hall of the rec center. I picture my keys on an aluminum chair in the depository, which is where I have bunked for the past several evenings. In fact, apart from the T-shirt, shorts, and flip-flops I don, all of my possessions are on the opposite side of that damn door. An awful feeling brews in the pit of my stomach. It's 12:30 AM, and my night is only getting started.

I make tracks to the neighboring kitchen. I tear to the passage beyond the storage area. The rear access is immovable to boot. I take many trips to the scullery for knives, hoping to

MacGyver into the room by sliding a blade in the crack between the knob and jamb. Nothing works. Out of ideas, I enter the shadowy gymnasium.

All lights are off. I don't want to wake the undergrads, so I patter on the parquet to their teacher. I tap him on the shoulder.

"Nick," I whisper. "Nick."

His eyes snap open with surprise.

"Can I use your phone?"

"Uh," he utters with confusion. "Sure."

Yawning, he slips me his mobile. I sneak back to the front.

In the mess hall, I realize the local contacts are on my cell, which is resting on my unreachable pillow. And of course I don't have any digits memorized. I'm to bother Nick once more when the sight of our white passenger van, visible by way of the cafeteria windows, catches me. My team leader materials are tucked under the driver's seat. Perhaps I didn't lock that door. I bolt.

I shove the front entry open, and the 30-degree temps almost shove me back in. I scamper to the Ford Transit. It's unlocked! I snatch my binder. I rush to the lunchroom.

I ring Devin, the individual in charge of the building. I leave a message. I also text him. Next, I dial the non-emergency number of the police. The guy on the line hasn't a clue what to do. He promises to call if he figures something out. The apathy in his voice, however, convinces me that we'll speak no more. I decide to revisit the gym.

Nick is soon brainstorming with me in the commissary. He surfs for locksmiths on his screen. Unfortunately, the nearest is twenty-five miles away, closed until 6:30 AM. I dial nonetheless and merely hear voicemail. Nick then trails me to the rear corridor, researching methods to undo security hinges. I reattempt to break into the depository with a variety of cooking utensils. I proceed to drag a stool over, stand on it, and lift the ceiling tile. Maybe I can scale the wall. I immediately learn, though, that the cement partition touches the roof. Stepping down, I ask Nick if I can keep his mobile in case Devin buzzes. Nick nods. I thank him for his help and suggest he nod off. He rapidly reappears to give me his extra blanket. He turns in for good.

I dart for the rec room. Unlike the plastic seats in the mess hall, those in the parlor at least have fabric. But a folding metal gate blocks access to the lounge via the complex's central foyer. So I hustle out the front, move left, and sprint a hundred feet to the first pair of double glass doors. One positive about leaving the key in my room is that there was no manner for me to secure this wing.

Eager to languish in the lounge for a bit, I pull three chairs together. I lay across them. I curl beneath my quilt. I try Devin again. I hear the answering machine again. It's 2:30 AM. I schedule an alarm for six o'clock. I place the cell on the pool table. My lids grow heavier and heavier.

A grating sound pops my peepers wide open a little later. I practically have a heart attack when I see a disheveled intruder glaring at me. His stocking cap stops just above his brows. He's grabbing the bars of the folding gate.

"You need to lock the lobby!" he scolds.

"I can't!" I angrily reply. "Do you have keys?!"

The drifter, who is swimming in his jacket and jeans, floats down the hall with no response. He veers right. He vanishes into the gymnasium.

I leap up. I burst outside and run to the main entry. It won't budge! I pound and pound on the glass, yet nobody comes. I start to shiver. My athletic tee and shorts are inadequate. Panic sets in. I must beeline to the game room ASAP. If the stranger latches those doors before I get back in, I'll freeze … either among the cedar trees or in a van with no heat. I hotfoot it. I burst through the threshold just seconds ahead of the boogeyman rounding the corner. Standing in the vestibule, I poke my noggin out from behind the glass.

"Can you please open the lobby?" I huff.

"I don't have keys."

"How did you lock it?"

"From the inside," he sneers.

He must have barred the entrance and then exited the edifice by means of the gym.

"Do you know who has the key?"

He shakes his skull.

"You trapped me in here," I assert. "How am I supposed to get to the rest of the building?!"

"Well, you will have to wait for someone."

He walks to his idling station wagon close by. He speeds away without hesitation.

It's 4:45, and my adrenaline is pumping. No chance I'm sleeping now. I cancel my alarm. I pace about the parlor, trying Devin various times. He finally answers at 5:40.

Devin, who appears he could pick up his pickup, arrives in approximately thirty minutes. He isn't mad I've left his skeleton in the storage closet, but he is confused by my report of the nocturnal visitor. He doesn't know anyone fitting my description of the ghostly dude.

"Ogema Security must send him here to check on things," Devin concludes.

He removes the padlock from the metal gate. We follow the main corridor to the storage room. He goes directly to the rear hall. He takes a stab at the back access with the kitchen knives I've already used. He glances at the ceiling tiles. He faces me.

"Thought of that," I admit.

He hurries to his truck. He returns with a hammer. He drags a stool over, sits on it, and tries mightily to pry the door with the claw. He slouches in disgust. Rising up, he approaches me, and raises the hammer as if to strike me.

"Come here!" he jokes. "I'm calling Ted."

A rusty SUV pulls up at 6:40. Ted, who sports a buzz cut and coveralls, enters the building. Devin points to the storage room. Ted saunters over, reaches in his pocket, and instantly opens the depository with his master. He grins at me.

"There you go," the janitor states with a smirk.

"You're lucky he lives close," Devin adds from across the cafeteria.

Ted and Devin engage in small talk. Two gals suddenly emerge, peering through the sand in their baby blues. They are lugging their duffels, sleeping bags, and deflated air mattresses. They are ready for the ride to Minneapolis.

"Tyrel, why haven't you changed yet?" one of them inquires.

She is clearly puzzled. In truth, I've normally been prepared for each day well before anybody else.

"Long story," I offer.

I quickly thank Ted and Devin. I zip to my room. We are to leave soon, and I have to change, pack, and help load the Ford. It's 6:45, and my adrenaline is still pumping.

I'm alone inside forty-five minutes later. Like the unexpected guest had done earlier, I secure the entrance and exit via the gym doors at the rear of the facility. Pavement leads me around a corner. I pass the lounge. The packed Transit awaits me. I climb in. I squint at Nick, who is riding shotgun.

"I appreciated the blanket and phone."

"Happy to help."

I turn the key. I put my hands atop the wheel. My bloodshot eyes stare into the dark dining hall of the rec center. I breathe deeply into the pit of my stomach. It's 7:30 AM—last night never ended—and my four-hour drive is only getting started.

18

Just Before Eight in Central Mexico

It's just before 8 PM when Héctor abruptly veers his white van onto the dusty shoulder. Hermanos Serdán International—our dimly lit destination—haunts us from across the interstate. We are so close that my accomplice could probably reach beyond his side mirror to tap the glass facade for which we set out forty minutes ago. I squint at the rearview. The glowing illumination of Puebla has faded away. Moreover, I do not detect the cherries and berries of a cop car, ambulance, or firetruck. Observing only obscurity, I have no idea why we have pulled up lame barely short of the finish line. My concern has a rapid growth spurt.

"¿Qué hace, Héctor?" I ask. *What are you doing, Héctor?*

"No quiero pagar el estacionamiento," he answers. *I don't want to pay for parking.* "Es caro." *It's expensive.*

Noticing that my brows are about to spring off my forehead, he further explains that the airport police will make us move if we hang at the hangar longer than it takes to shift into park. Our soon-to-be passengers must be observed wheeling their luggage toward our back doors for us to remain curbside.

"¿Cuándo van a llegar?" Héctor inquires. *When are they going to arrive?*

"A las ocho … supuestamente." *At 8:00 … supposedly.*

I can't ignore the clock on the center console. The digital numbers sluggishly advance on that dark, lonely highway in central Mexico. And I can't shake the shakes in the passenger seat. Perhaps the chills I feel are due to the fifty-degree temps fogging up the windshield. Or the quivers could very well be the nerves I always get prior to receiving volunteers. I am on the verge of meeting a group of eleven from Carroll University after all. The wait is wearing on me. I wriggle. I lean forward. I slouch. I simply can't find a comfortable way to sit. Nor can

I decide if my watch should go on my right or left wrist. At last, a cluster of lights emerges in the sky. I watch it slowly descend behind the terminal.

"Por fin han llegado," I sigh. *They have finally arrived.*

"Sí, pero todavía tienen que pasar por la aduana," Héctor adds. *Yes, but they still have to pass through customs.*

Our shoulders slump simultaneously. Our concurrent, conquered chuckles accompany the air abandoning the auto. Little did I know, though, that the deplaning individuals we'd eventually pick up would lift me up for the next week and a half.

A four-hour ride with Héctor the following day took us from Puebla to Cuetzalan. The ten undergrads, their professor, and I hit the cobblestones running once we stepped off the van and into the green confines of Hotel Taselotzin. During the daze to come, we dug into our service project in the nearby village of Xiloxochico (She-low-show-cheek-oh). The task was to clear the righthand section of a two-room structure overlooking the playground of Bachillerato José Vasconcelos—the local high school. This simple-sounding endeavor, however, proved to be quite challenging.

With shovels, pickaxes, buckets, and wheelbarrows, our team labored alongside area students and parents to gradually remove a mound of dirt—several feet high and wide— from the future library. The soil primarily consisted of stubborn clay and rocks. The job site was sodden thanks to the relentless January rains. Those who participated in the bucket brigades above the miners were at risk of falling into the excavation area. The wheelbarrow path was narrow, slippery, and steep. Biting bugs constantly launched attacks from the overturned earth to boot, so workers were frequently swatting at the napes of their necks. In addition, those wearing short sleeves were continuously slapping their arms. We remained steadfast nonetheless, hurdling these obstacles to ultimately finish the dig. We even had enough remaining in the tank to transport blocks (for the walls one day) across the playground to the base of the hill upon which the impending book repository stood.

But our purpose in Xilo wasn't solely to help build a library. Throughout the week, we used the undertaking as the means to form relationships with the locals and the students and staff of the high school. We spent a lot of time playing UNO, soccer, basketball, and guitar. We broke bread, exchanged many laughs, and posed together for countless pictures. These occasions we shared with community members far outweighed the perpetual pails of mud we hauled. Therefore, the Carroll crew and I found it hard to bid farewell to our new friends, and, in particular, our motherly Nahua guide, Victoria Contreras Coyota.

Because Doña Viky had accompanied us for the entirety of our journey in Cuetzalan, not to mention her native Xiloxochico, she had trouble uttering adios, too. I caught the sadness in her face while our squad had a Kodak moment with her in front of our ecolodge. Like most of us, her eyes welled up shortly after our final photo, and I tried to grasp how difficult it must have been for her to see us leave. Doña Viky treated us as an extension of her family. In fact, she was with us more than her actual family. Given that she prepared our breakfasts and dinners in Cuetzalan, she bunked at Hotel Taselotzin rather than make the tedious commute to Xilo every evening. It was only natural for her to become attached to the people she took under her wing. I begin to comprehend this connection two mornings later.

It's just before 8 AM when I abruptly leave my seat to hug the Carroll University group, who are in line to board their plane to the States. While I take in each of my teammates entering the jet bridge, I think back on the whirlwind adventure we have experienced. A somber smile appears on my face. Flashes of our trip suddenly flood my mind.

I recollect my fellow travelers' falls in misty forests, out of vehicles, and on the soccer pitch. I remember them falling ill, being homesick, and at times noticeably down. Yet I also recall them getting down on the dance floor at Disco Toca Toca (Cuetzalan's hotspot), then dirty on the job site. This reminds me of extremely sore muscles, which don't get any better as we shiver during dinner at Hotel Taselotzin. I reflect upon our attempt to fight a chilly eve at the inn by entering the torrid Temazcal. In the sweat lodge we swelter a river and subsequently follow one to a beautiful waterfall—Cascada Las Brisas. Reminiscing on our hike to the lagoon conjures up our closing climb mere hours ago. Atop the roof of Hotel Colonial, we witness Puebla brilliantly irradiate the midnight sky. All these vivid images have made it tough for me to say goodbye.

My flight to Houston doesn't depart for a while, but I can't sit. Instead, I am pulled toward the windows looming over the tarmac. I can't take my eyes off their plane. I watch it slowly ascend behind the clouds.

Doña Viky and the team in front of Hotel Taselotzin. Cuetzalan, Puebla, Mexico, January 2018.

19

Memories of Mom and Mexico

To say my mother had a green thumb would be a drastic understatement. It was more like she had fertilizer fingers—whatever she put in the ground was bound to thrive. My early boyhood yard starred sunflowers that towered over Mom's four feet eleven inches. When I was a teenager, I'd often catch our cats lying low in her flourishing labyrinth of hostas, honeysuckles, and hydrangeas. As an adult, there was never a doubt she would give me a tour of her tomatoes and tulips when I visited. Yet the appearance of my mom's gardens isn't all I remember. By watching her labor on the Minnesotan soil all those years, I knew that her pristine plots didn't come easy. She showed me that people must grind to get great results. She also taught me to put forth my best through the endless hours, effort, and attentiveness she invested in her flowerbeds. She exemplified the art of being present to boot. My mother simply loved to be on the lawn, literally taking time to smell the roses while she faithfully watered them. These images lately remind me of an impactful journey I experienced with some other remarkable women a couple of years ago.

It's a muggy morn in mid-June when the van suddenly stops.

"¿Nos bajamos?" I ask with wide eyes. *We're getting out?*

My Mexican seatmate nods. "Y ahora caminamos." *And now we walk.*

The vehicle can't traverse the steep track ahead. It may be the end of the road for the combi but not for its six passengers. A pair of mother-daughter pairs (an adventurous duo from Canada and a tenacious twosome from the U.S.) and I hop out to hoof it alongside Doña Viky. She confidently leads the team of volunteers deeper into the verdant highlands of the Sierra Norte.

The humidity hangs onto me like a hiking pack while slogging up and down the wooded slopes. My light green tee turns forest. Sharing in shouldering a five-gallon pail of exterior enamel causes my clothes to cling to me even more. My spirits are lifted, though, upon the site of a distant church to our right. But Doña Viky presses on without hesitation. A closer look reveals that the chapel is godforsaken … akin to my hopes of reaching our destination.

Twenty minutes in, I finally spot the final approach to Chicueyaco—a village of less than 400 residents that takes cover five kilometers northeast of Cuetzalan.

I don't yell. I don't run. These are the rules tattooed immediately below the gable of the pueblo's old and decrepit single-room preschool. They cannot be found on the drab bricks holding up the current Escuela Preescolar Benito Juárez, which is only thirty feet downhill from its rotting predecessor. I notice, however, that the puny pupils still meet these expectations when I poke my head through the open doorway. A handful of kids are sitting quietly as they contently color in their books. I then feel a tap on my shoulder. I turn around to find the all-female parents' committee staring at me.

"Están listas," Doña Viky asserts. *They are ready.*

"Bueno, entonces empecemos," I reply. *Well, let's start then.*

Ripping the plastic cap off the container of paint, I wonder why we didn't buy another.

"¿Es suficiente?" I question Doña Viky. *Is it enough?*

"Por supuesto. Mire." *Of course. Watch.*

Escuela Preescolar Benito Juárez, Chicueyaco, Cuetzalan del Progreso, Puebla, Mexico, June 2018

She lifts the heavy bucket and splashes some of the creamsicle coloring into an empty receptacle. She clutches a two-liter jug of water left by the brigade of local ladies, who are lugging liquid from the neighboring elementary, and dumps it onto the pigment she just poured. She cups her calloused hands and tosses a little more H2O into the mix. Picking up a long stick, she stirs until she knows the paint has the correct composition.

"Hay bastante," Doña Viky adds. *There is plenty.*

My fellow volunteers, half a dozen area women, and I grab for the brushes and rollers. Everyone is dripping. Everyone is determined. A well-oiled machine, the crew promptly coats the front of the building and gets the sides half covered by midday. Ladders will need to be built to hit the rest of the gray blocks on the rear of the preschool. Juana María Nicolasa Chepe, a longstanding community leader, requests that everybody gather round.

Doña Juanita gives a heartfelt speech. She affirms that the students, their parents, and the staff of the schoolhouse will benefit from the work that has been done today. First, they will have extra incentive to be involved with the institution because the fresh overlay shows that enhancement is taken seriously. Cantaloupe also provides a warm, inviting hue to those who view the structure from the outside. So hopefully nearby residents will be drawn to and subsequently support the establishment. She further states that this lively tone will surely make for a more dynamic learning environment once it is on the classroom walls. To conclude this emotional moment, a couple of the ladies who helped in the undertaking claim that they are proud to have had a role in the progress of Escuela Preescolar Benito Juárez. The positive energy floating around me could power the towns along the leafy valley.

Over 25 months have gone by since the paint dried. Nevertheless, I often think about that fiery Friday in the Puebla state … especially recently. Perhaps I mentally hike through the central Mexican mountains because the values demonstrated by the women there were also epitomized by Mom, who died a week before Mother's Day 2020.

Like my mom, the ladies in Chicueyaco took pride in their work. They regularly strategized prior to meticulously applying their brushstrokes to the cinder walls. They were persistent. The sun was unforgiving, yet the go-getters stayed the course until no more paint could be rolled. They were present. I continue to hear the jokesters' laughs while they slapped on coats. I never cease to see their grins in the numerous photos together. And I keep on getting goosebumps whenever I rehash Doña Juanita's moving message in my head.

I replay Mom's words, too. Memories flood my mind. I ignore my laptop to take in the living room plants she gave me several years back. A smile fights its way to the surface. They're still green as can be.

20

Time on the Line

Regret has been a main player in my grief. I wish I would have spent extra time with my mother. She lived almost an hour away, so it was hard for me to stop by during the workweek. I'd see her on weekends every now and then, but I should have seen her more regularly. I got wrapped up in my own life, though. Or, I put off visiting her because I assumed that I would have plenty of opportunities later. I kick myself for taking things for granted. In the few years before her death, however, my mom and I did chat quite a bit via the Bluetooth in my car. I am grateful for those conversations after those long nights on the job.

I taught Spanish courses to adults — two, three, even four evenings per week. Following the final bell, I regularly called Mom while I drove on dark, nearly empty interstates. Given that both of my schools were around 30 minutes from home, I believed this to be a solid window through which we could catch up. Here and there I would reveal my disappointments in regard to a lesson that backfired. And my mother would undoubtedly give me confidence boosters.

"You can't please everyone," she'd attest. "Just do your best. Your next class will go better."

She also frequently used our time on the line to express whatever frustrations she had. She was extremely loquacious, in fact. On countless occasions, her concerns would carry far beyond the highway exit sign. There were numerous instances when I was already parked in my garage, listening to my mom pour out her thoughts long after the light to the overhead door opener had clicked off.

My brother Jay was a reliable sounding board for Mom as well. I knew this because he and I would naturally compare our marathon telephone sessions. But my little bro and I were okay with lending our ears. We understood our mother's longwindedness.

"She just needs someone to talk to," my sibling would say.

My mom didn't have many outlets. She was often isolated, rarely venturing past her gardens due to her weakening condition. She didn't want to be on the road or the floor of a store if her body were to suddenly betray her, so she didn't leave the house unless necessary. Therefore, she mostly drove her SUV to pick up one of her umpteen medications from the pharmacy or to pop in Western Union to wire money to family in the Philippines. When her health further deteriorated, she ultimately turned off the ignition for good, contacting taxis or overpaying neighbors to take her to her usual haunts. Because her public appearances were few and far between, the phone was her primary method to connect with others.

Jay began his listening skills at an early age. Bloomington, Minnesota, January 1984. Photo by Beth Nelson.

In the months following her death, I caught myself inevitably acting like Mom. This was evident in my calls to my brother. As he did with our mother, Jay would answer his cell in Seattle to hear me ramble on and on about my latest letdowns. I'd finally recognize that I was doing what our mom did. I would imagine my bro calmly acknowledging her grievances all those years with the same "uh-huh" and "yup" he was repeatedly using with me.

"Thanks for letting me vent," I'd tell him.

"Any time," he'd confidently reply.

I also found myself really missing the late talks with Mom while I sat behind the wheel, especially the rides down memory lane. There were several landmarks along the route that served as triggers.

"Where are you right now?" my mother would ask me without fail.

"I'm heading south on 35W, coming up on 66th Street … right by Woodlake Nature Center."

"Oh, Dad and I used to take you and your brother there when you guys were little!"

In truth, she told me loads of stories—lots which will never be shared again (at least with such enthusiasm and vivid narration) now that she's gone. After my father breathed his last, my mom was the main memory keeper for Jay and me. She was the only one left who could describe certain parts of our family history, especially her first decade in Minnesota—the mid-70s to mid-80s. She would invariably go into great detail when she reflected upon the first snowfall she experienced, the first apartment she and Pop rented in Bloomington, not to mention the heart-pounding trips they had together while Mom was learning how to drive. Moreover, she loved to speak of the days that my bro and I were too young to remember. My sibling was a quick study according to her. And my first word was "dee-da" ("daddy" backwards), which always made her chuckle.

I miss her laughter. I miss her voice, which is why I listen to it on my phone. I immediately resave those old messages—so many have been forever lost. Nobody could recount an account like my mother. If only I could have saved those stories, too. Damn regrets.

21

On the Verge

I was in high school, fully committed to the air solo of a Metallica number, when I suddenly caught an effect hidden behind the music blasting from my speakers. I did not remember laughs being on this track. Nor did I realize that I had left my bedroom door open. The cackles continued. I spun around. My mom was on the verge of tears. I still feel my cheeks getting warm after twenty-some years.

I jam a lot—for real—now. I strum away every day to temporarily escape the profoundness of my mother's departure. It doesn't take long before my concentration is broken nonetheless. Memories cause me to strike a wrong chord or forget the next one completely. Pausing to regain focus, I page through my three-ring binder of songs until I find a piece to sink my teeth into. I stretch my fingers for a stretch. I choose an acoustic. Otherwise, I crank my amp. No matter the tune, however, I can't seem to tune her out.

"Your father said he felt like getting up and dancing when he heard you play," Mom often told me after Pop passed away.

The sadness of such statements nearly sits me down. Shiftlessness stabs me more, though. Bleakness bombards my brain if I am not occupied, so I pluck on for a spell. My right shoulder begins to burn. My left forearm starts on fire.

"You need to take breaks!" is all I can hear during the onset of these pains.

Heeding the advice of my physical therapists, I close the case on my black or brown classical. Or, I unplug my Fender Stratocaster. I normally head to the kitchen for a snack. Yet this action hasn't been much of a distraction either.

The cupboards are replete with reminiscence. The crackers and cookies remind me of the goodies my mom consistently insisted that I take with me prior to hitting the road. Moreover, I reflect upon how her doggedness sometimes got my goat.

"Your mother mentioned that you were mad at her because she wanted you to take the cake," my dad once brought up to me on the phone.

"Yeah," I admitted. "I can't eat all that food. Plus, I don't have anywhere to put it!"

"You're her son, Tyrel," he replied in an annoyed tone. "She's just trying to take care of you."

I retaste the guilt I swallowed as I hung up. I further recollect waking up in the middle of the night to devour the dessert Mom had worn me down with mere hours earlier.

On a shelf next to the stove, the CorningWare my mom gave to Alyssa and me a couple of years ago never fails to catch my eye. Not only do I flash on how proud she was to give us the ceramics, but also how set she was on shipping my brother an identical set. She regularly checked in about the cookware to boot.

"So, what's for dinner?" my mother routinely asked me. "Does my daughter like using the dishes I gave you guys?"

The glass containers in another cabinet make me ponder the automatic jar opener Mom would undoubtedly employ to uncap them. A proponent of the gadget, it was no surprise that she wrapped one for Alyssa and me some Christmases back. I also recall smiling while discovering the device in my mom's pantry after she died.

The plant in the corner of the kitchen conjures up images of my mother, too. She tidied up the golden pothos the last time she was in my home. In fact, I frequently dwell upon that day in October when she promptly pulled the dead leaves from each of my houseplants, which were actually hers before she literally handed them to me several years back.

"Make sure you do this once in a while," she urged as she swiftly snatched the perished petals.

I naturally shift my gaze through the window above the golden pothos. Watching the squirrels tightrope the brown picket fence between the house and garage, I occasionally think of the baby rodent Mom tried to raise almost two decades ago. She found the infant under a tree in her garden, pink and clinging to life. She nursed the newborn back to health, feeding it salt and sugar water with a dropper. The squirrel shot up, grew a thick gray coat, and became so comfortable with my mom that it would even sit on her shoulder. She kept the pet for a bit … until it bit her. She subsequently released her furry child into the wild.

The lawn slowly grows wild if I contemplate the backyard for a moment. Convincing myself that it's close enough to a week since the previous snip, I usually jump at the chance to cut the grass. The edger on the weed wacker satisfies my meticulousness. I become engrossed in mowing perfectly straight rows. And for roughly 60 precious minutes, the self-propelled engine muffles the apathetic and disingenuous comments made to me about my mother's death over the past few months. The sanity-saving yardwork is great, but, above all, the Toro links me to Mom in yet another way. She gave the lawnmower to me as well.

The connections continue. My mind spins around. And I'm always on the verge of tears.

Escaping in my living room. Richfield, Minnesota, December 2020. Photo by Alyssa Nelson.

22

Final Order

Mom used to take my brother and me with her to a Filipino supermarket when we were kids. Our mother was a frequent customer, so she was a familiar face in the mom-and-pop shop. Visits tended to be quite lengthy since Mom would take a while to chat with those she encountered while she perused the produce. Jay and I didn't care nonetheless. In truth, we were occupied with navigating an intriguing labyrinth that offered shelves and shelves of sauces and spices, barricades of 50-pound rice bags, as well as nooks full of noodles. If we weren't racing along the aisles, my little bro and I were normally frozen in the seafood section, entranced by the barrels of live crabs. Their antennae were alluring. Their claws were captivating. Their puny peepers were perplexing. Additionally, our mother often purchased a bucket or two of the crustaceans, which kept Jay and me entertained the entire way home … and then some.

"Oh my gosh!" our mom yelled upon returning from the grocery store one afternoon.

Investigating her exclamation, my brother and I entered the kitchen to notice a pail on its side and Mom on her knees. She was trying to recapture the many crabs that were crawling laterally across the linoleum. Suddenly, I was afraid of their approaching antennas, petrified by their pincers, and too scared to glance into their black, deathlike eyes. My mother, on the other hand, was unfazed. She scooped up the crustaceans and put them back in their container without hesitation. The next moment I saw the crabs they were on a serving plate.

Three decades later, I discovered several crates of plates under my mom's guest bed. She just didn't have the time or energy to ship them before she died. Yet I knew where the dishes, not to mention the effects stashed around them, were supposed to go. As far as I could remember, Mom had been sending things (e.g., clothes, toys, toiletries) to family in the

Philippines. She was constantly looking out for the people she loved, no matter the distance, so it was common to see gifts stockpiled throughout the house. If the articles were not hanging in a wardrobe, or heaped on a closet floor, they were already stored in stacks of jumbo corrugated boxes, which were layered in clear packing tape. The packages would disappear regularly. Nevertheless, they were usually replaced rather quickly by new parcels awaiting pickup from the local Filipino delivery service. Not only was forwarding this freight important to my mother, but it was also urgent to me now. I had to keep my word.

"Don't worry," I assured my mom during one of our last talks. "I'll take care of everything."

It was this promise which had me inspecting Mom's possessions the morning after she passed away. Considering I was grief stricken, it was difficult for me to concentrate. I'd abruptly stop whatever I was doing because I frequently daydreamed. Attempting to crack the chaos in my coconut, I was dumbfounded by how fast my world had changed. I couldn't believe my mother had been admitted to hospice care merely three weeks earlier. Moreover, I thought about how extra challenging this stretch had been due to the COVID-19 restrictions. She at least tested negative for the coronavirus—watching her suffer from kidney disease was agonizing enough. I was also fortunate to be allowed near her bedside (provided the nurse or home health aide were not in her personal space). Unfortunately, I couldn't do much else. I really struggled with the fact that I couldn't be as supportive as I had wanted for fear of transmitting the virus. I couldn't hug her. I couldn't hold her hand. I couldn't even pull down my N95 mask to show her a smile. Having to maintain my distance from my dying mom sickened my heart. Going through what she left behind broke it.

Anything I touched in her place triggered nostalgia. The knick-knacks I swaddled in newspaper reminded me of how Mom always had dolls on almost every bookcase, tabletop, and shelf in sight. The random pockets of change I dug out of old jackets and jeans made me recall how she regularly collected coins. She would load china teapots with meter money, but wouldn't spend the silver on parking. Instead, she saved the coinage to pay the young neighbor boy who lived across the street from her during her final years to tend her garden. And the dusty Polaroid camera I uncovered forced me to flash on my high school graduation. I was walking down a hallway to the gymnasium with a group of classmates when my mother appeared out of nowhere to take a pre-ceremony snapshot.

Thankfully, Alyssa was there to snap me out of my head trips. She pushed the project ahead to boot. Naturally thinking in advance, my number one could predict the number of boxes needed for each room. So she would keep me moving by asking me to tape up and hand her some cardboard upon request. If I wasn't constructing the cases, I would help her prepare the cargo for a two-month journey on the Pacific. She invariably knew how to wrap the items surrounding us, regardless of their fragility. I would have been packing for God knows how long without her.

All in all, Alyssa and I devoted three whole days to stuffing 12 boxes bound for the Philippines. Twelve was a good amount. A baker's dozen, however, would have been unacceptable. Appreciating my mom's superstitiousness, I would have wrangled whatever it took to send 14 packages. Honoring Mom's selflessness, my wife and I subsequently donated most of the remaining belongings to an area nonprofit.

The rooms were practically bare when I located a laundry basket brimming with documents. Slowly sifting through the layers of papers, I eventually uncovered Jay's and my childhood. Report cards, certificates of achievement, and school portraits from every grade filled the bottom half of the bin. I even spotted my baby book. Teary-eyed, I carefully read each beige page. The last entry, which was penned back in the daze of the supermarket maze, hit me the hardest.

Hi! Tyrel is now 10 years old, and did lots of great things that made me and his dad very proud of him.

My mother's words sunk in. I hoped completing her final order made her proud, too. I further hoped she knew how incredibly proud I was to call her my mom.

23

Walking Ahead

While my mom's condition declined in her last decade, she tried her best to stay active. She swam at the YMCA during strokes of improved health. She attended yoga classes for a stretch. She pushed through weeks of physical therapy at home just months before she turned up her toes. Her most common form of exercise, however, was walking. Weather permitting, she strolled the streets near her place—even if it was simply to check the community mailbox or drop off her lot rent at the office.

"I am going to miss Beth," the trailer park manager said when I called to inform her of my mother's passing. "I enjoyed talking to her whenever she popped in."

On the other hand, Mom wore out her carpet if the elements were unforgiving. She shuffled back and forth along the entire length of her single-wide if outdoor activity wasn't an option.

I do plenty of indoor laps myself these days. My anxiety gets the better of me at times, so I move around to spend the nervous energy festering within. I nonetheless attempt to be helpful as I battle the butterflies in my stomach. I throw tiny loads into the washer. I empty trash cans which are half full. I give once-overs to areas that Alyssa recently cleaned. Regardless of the invented chore, though, I frequently become lost in dreams of yesteryear while on my feet. It's not rare for me to enter a room and forget why I am standing there with my palms up. This confusion is representative of the overall turmoil which has been tearing me up inside since my mom died. To be honest, the distress I have felt as I navigate the new normal without my mother has often stopped me in my tracks. I ponder the past. Powerful images rule my thoughts.

I am in the back of my dad's crimson Plymouth Horizon. Junior sits in the front passenger seat. Senior is focusing on the green light ahead. We are in the middle of the intersection when an explosion suddenly blasts us sideways. Screeching, spinning, and shattering glass is all I hear. The world finally stops whirling, and my vision clears to reveal the traffic light pole dividing the car's grill. My pop is hunched to the left with his fingers locked behind his neck. Little brother is holding his throat. My right ear is on fire.

Jay (front) and I waiting for Dad to get into the Horizon in the late 1980s. Photo by Beth Nelson.

I am soon seated beside my father on the curb. He can't recite our address, or any contact info for that matter, so I fill in the blanks for the cops. Jay has been swiftly wheeled away. The siren from his ambulance fades fast while the approaching alarms get louder and louder. The young man who broadsided us slinks into view, providing shade from the hot August sun. He apologizes profusely. I later discover he and his girlfriend were locking horns instead of locking eyes on the signal which had turned red.

The next thing I know, I am on a hospital bed. Mom bursts into my room. She repeatedly runs her hand from my forehead to crown. Her comfort abruptly unleashes the emotions I have been holding in all afternoon. I start to cry. Yet my waterworks are not due to the pain of the shard that sliced my ear open. Watching my thirteen-year-old life flash before my eyes has utterly shaken me. I am also worried about Dad, who couldn't remove his hands from his nape. And I am scared for my sibling. I have no idea where he is.

"How's Jay?!" I ask in a panic.

"He needed 20 stitches," my mom replies. "He's very lucky the glass didn't cut deeper."

"How's Pop?!"

"His neck really hurts, but he'll be okay."

Spotting my tears causes my mother to shed her own. They stream down her cheeks and splash onto mine over and over again.

Sadly, summoning up these sobs eventually connects me to a rather regretful memory. I remember many years ago when Mom phoned me bawling; she had learned her brother Jun in the Philippines had succumbed to cancer. But I failed her. My words were awfully limited. I wasn't sure what to say because I was a self-centered twentysomething who avoided the topic of death. And since I was too uncomfortable speaking on the subject, the condolences and questions ended once we hung up. I didn't continue to check on my mom afterwards like I should have. I didn't call to see how she was coping with the departure of her loved one. Nor did I ask her to tell me more about the uncle who I had only met briefly.

Such stinging recollections nevertheless shape my present. I now live determined to be a more considerate person, perhaps subconsciously trying to compensate for the areas in which I fell short with my mother. I make the conscious effort to be an active listener to those who are struggling with loss. In addition, I do my utmost to not only touch base on occasion, yet I also remind them that I am just around the corner if needed.

Mom is close, too. As unsettling as being unemployed during a pandemic has been, I use the map she has given me while I look down the road. I relive our last deep conversation. I still hear her final piece of advice.

"Be strong, my son," she asserted. "Good surprises will come if you stay true to yourself."

My mom was always true to herself. In fact, I think of the courage required for her to refuse dialysis as the end neared, despite the urging of others. She wasn't afraid of dying. She didn't want to further torture her body merely to add a tick to the tail of her journey either. Her fearlessness at this profoundly vulnerable moment inspires me to bravely take on any challenge which comes across my path. I have a great example to follow. I know she'll be walking with me each step of the way.

24

Rambling to Reassurance

My heart hit the floor the instant I saw my mother. She was skin and bones, not much thicker than the blankets keeping her warm in her hospice bed. Her chest pronouncedly rose and fell to the slow beat of her labored breath. Tears dripped down the edges of my N95 mask. I stood at the foot of her cot, realizing the woman who brought me into this world would soon leave it. The seconds were suddenly sacred. It was April 25. I was doubtful Mom was going to make it to May. When she sadly made eye contact with me, I was sure she was unsure as well.

My mom grew weaker over the ensuing week. My greatest fear was that she was scared. For this reason, I was at her side each day, trying my best to give her a little comfort and familiarity. I held my cell to her face so she could do daily video chats with my brother in Seattle and her work daughter in New Orleans. I prepared her tea with multiple packets of sugar—just how she liked it. I also dedicated our conversations to making certain her wishes would be met. However, her lids got heavier and heavier until she could look at my screen no more. The cups on her bedside table went from empty to full. We shifted from deep discussion to small talk to simply "I love you." In truth, that was the last phrase I uttered to her on the evening of May 2. She mumbled three syllables back to me. She passed away shortly ahead of the next sunrise.

The rest of the month was restless for me. I frequently relived my final hours with my mother. I repeatedly assured her that I would tie up any loose ends.

"It's alright, Mom," I would say. "Everything will be okay."

I was therefore consumed with fulfilling my promise. I first ensured that my mom was cremated. I picked up her ashes in the haze to follow. Advised to take her to a special place to ultimately spread her cremains with my brother, I choose an urn that Jay deemed suitable. It displayed a beautiful sunset over the ocean. In addition, I closed my mother's accounts, which was awful. Mourning was very difficult in and of itself. But always encountering apathy while aiming to square all in the name of Elizabeth Acaton Nelson made me want to throw my phone against the wall.

The month of June was a month of gloom. No longer occupied with handling Mom's affairs, the despair started to devour me from the inside out. I was exhausted. Regret over time lost ravaged my thoughts. Agonizing images of those last eight days—helplessly watching my mom convert her living room to a dying room—kept me up at night. Although I really appreciated those who sent me caring messages, I was extremely disappointed overall. People who I expected to contact me failed to do so. Others were too eager to turn my heartache into a chance to chat about a distant loss of their own. The remaining gave disingenuous, seemingly obligatory condolences. Their comments were often succeeded by insensitive questions, such as "Did she die of old age?". I was also alone. Being parentless at 40 sent me to solitary confinement because I had no one to relate to. I felt cheated. Everybody I knew around the same age still had their mother or father—most had both. I consequently began grief counseling to sort my emotions.

Be that as it may, June's sleeplessness carried into July. I focused on the few activities through which I could channel my anxiety. I exercised regularly. I jumped rope, jogged, and practically ran out of fitness videos on my TV. I played my guitars till the early hours. I learned many tunes strumming away before the break of dawn. Moreover, music reconnected me with Mom, who filled our house with her robust renditions of Patsy Cline songs during my childhood. And akin to what my mom did in her score of journals, which I discovered after she died, I put pen to paper to process my perceptions. I was initially convinced I inherited my writing from Dad, who constantly scribbled words on whatever scrap he could find. It was nonetheless eye-opening to see that I shared this outlet with my mother to boot. I never knew…

I didn't know what to do with myself once August arrived. COVID-19 stifled the org I was working for—so much so I was let go. This extra free time just caused my mind to wander more. I stumbled down the backstretch of summer, solely directed by ways to honor Mom's memory. An important step was to celebrate her birthday.

It is August 25. I am doubtful I am going to make it through midday. The 90-degree temp is intolerable. I hustle to the entrance of the Lakewood Garden Mausoleum. The AC is a life saver. My body temp immediately lowers while I descend the stairs to marble town. The crypt is spick and span. Light pours through ceiling windows and the tall panes forming the building's south facade. The only sound is my amplified breathing, which is bouncing off the borders of my face covering. Countless cards and flowers decorate the hall of chiseled names. I pass half of them prior to standing below my mom's. I stare at Elizabeth Acaton Nelson, who is high on the memorial wall, for a bit. Her plaque provides the backdrop for four decades of mental pictures playing in my head. I eventually tell my mother I miss her before pushing a nearby exit door.

Despite the humidity, I am grounded to these verdant grounds. They remind me of

Mom. She would dig this heat, in fact. She grew up in the tropics, so she'd totally be in her element at the moment. I smile remembering how she usually tested the upper limits of the thermostat during the winter. My grin widens when I recall how Alyssa continually informs me that it's too hot in the house. I can visualize my mom tending the thriving gardens around me. Circling the large reflection pool, I think about the vast body of water she crossed to begin a new life with my pop in Minnesota. I ponder how painful it must have been for her to leave her family in the Philippines. I ponder how painful it has been since she left those who loved her stateside. I wonder how peaceful her current home is now that she is no longer in pain.

Comforted by this belief, I let my breath out for the first time in forever. I stroll for several minutes, taking in my tranquil surroundings. I am quickly compelled to visit my mother again. I reenter the mausoleum. I proudly look at her marker.

"It's alright, Mom," I say. "I'll be okay."

Reflection pool at Lakewood Cemetery. Minneapolis, Minnesota, August 2020.

25

Checking In

During the months following my dad's death, I regularly toured a local park which he and I used to frequent. I wore out my sneakers not only to clear my melancholy mind but also to be close to my best friend. I was lost without him. However, I continued to ask Pop for advice like I did previous to his passing. It didn't matter if he was no longer physically beside me atop the asphalt track. I still felt better after talking to him.

On a drizzly morning that April, I was again seeking calmness and counsel at the recreation area when an unfamiliar snout suddenly snagged my attention. As soon as I stepped out of my truck, a spry black lab came running in my direction from the other end of the parking lot, which was approximately the length of a softball field. I initially assumed the owner was behind me, yet I heard no calls for the sprinter. I spun and spotted no one. I glanced right, but no one was in sight. I turned to the opposite shoulder. Nobody was left. The hound was getting closer and closer. We locked eyes—there was no doubt the stray was galloping my way. My confusion morphed into trepidation. I had never seen this animal and, therefore, had no idea what would develop once we met. I soon realized my shock was wasted energy. The pooch simply wanted to be patted. I obliged for a minute or two before heading for the trailhead.

Fido tailed me anyhow. I could hear his paws quickly slapping the wet pavement behind me. Deciding my somber soul could use the company, I stopped to let my new buddy catch up. And I was glad I did. I was comforted by the pup's companionship while we traversed the rest of the trail together. I wasn't so lonely and depressed. I looked forward instead of at my shoes this time.

"Can I pet your dog?" a passerby inquired near the halfway mark.

"Uh, he's not my dog." I responded with a chuckle.

The guy roared. "Have you seen *The Pink Panther Strikes Again*?"

I immediately understood his reference. Laughing with me about the bite scene in the hotel lobby, the older fellow patted my partner on the base of his neck prior to moving on.

Reaching my Ranger, I crouched to pet my protector for a bit. I really didn't want to leave my sidekick. I couldn't drive the rover home either. So I scanned the area to see if any panicky owners were coming into view. No dice. I didn't know what to do. The doggy did nevertheless. Possibly sensing I wasn't going to leave until he was safe and sound, the hound backed up a few steps. Then he confidently stared at me for several seconds. My pal swiftly turned around and dashed into the distance, disappearing as fast as he had appeared a half hour earlier.

Putting the park in my rearview, I recalled my father periodically mentioning the black lab he had in the early 1970s. He spoke quite highly of the canine, invariably highlighting her loyalty and especially her IQ. Thinking of Dad's puppy made me dwell upon the one I just saw. I further pondered how his presence lifted me up like my pop did during my slumps … in a place important to both of us. I eventually came to the conclusion that, on this day, man's best friend was my best friend making certain I was alright.

Wood Lake Nature Center, Richfield, Minnesota, October 2020

According to my mom, my father was still checking on me nine years later. While she lay in her living room, she told me of the chats she was having with her ex-husband in her dreams. I had no reason not to trust her either. I had had my share of REM convos with him since his departure.

"Are you getting any sleep, Son?" my mother asked.

"Not really," I answered.

"Your dad is worried about you," she added. "He says you need to take care of yourself."

"I know," I replied. "I'm here to focus on you, though."

"Don't jeopardize your health because of me," she insisted.

Pop would say that. In fact, he uttered the same statement to me when he, too, was in hospice care.

But it was totally in Mom's nature to also express her concern. She had always looked out for me. Fighting back the tears I detected in the reflection of her muted TV, I considered the many things she had done for me. I remembered her giving my brother and me meticulous haircuts during our childhood. The appointments usually lasted an hour or two, yet the dapper dos were worth the wait. I went back to eighth grade and, subsequently, the whole slew of afternoons she picked me up from baseball practice. This reminded me of the games she attended the following summer, more than any other. I regretted my college years. I hated how my smart-alecky, know-it-all, self-absorbed persona took her for granted. There were countless instances when I stopped by my mom's place, which was only 15 to 20 minutes north of the University of Minnesota, requesting she use her unmatched sewing skills to fix my clothes. She often ironed them to boot. And fed me. She did so much for me. I should have thanked her a lot more before she died.

In the months since my mother cashed in her chips, I have kept my eyes peeled and ears open so I wouldn't miss her attempts to contact me. I have faith that she's trying. While Mom walked in this world, she firmly maintained her connectedness to the one beyond. Granting I never witnessed the spirits she brought up on occasion, some of her actions I observed, such as conversing with tombstones, were rather convincing. The revealing reports from her hospice bed attached extra weight to her words. Her updates on my father were powerful. In addition, she described the exchanges she had with other loved ones, who were awaiting her arrival during her final windows of lucidity.

In truth, I feel my mom has poked at me through the porthole every now and then. I recognize these nudges whenever inexplicable waves of tranquility abruptly wash over me at my lowest points. I hold that this is her means of telling me that everything will be okay. The most recent occurrence happened as I was dragging my feet at Wood Lake—a nature center we would visit together when I was a little boy. Perhaps she was the random Milkwood seed I saw helicoptering over me upon entering the reserve. Maybe she was the whistle I heard rustling the canopy above while I hiked the dirt trails. And it could have been her embrace I sensed around my shoulders under the surprisingly warm autumn sun. Although a pup hasn't randomly appeared to perk me up, I believe my mother is still checking on me in some fashion. I'll make sure to thank her the next time we cross paths … no matter her shape or form.

Wood Lake Nature Center, Richfield, Minnesota, October 2020

Afterword

I was just 11 or 12 when I went to my mom's company picnic. I can't say what I ate, who I spoke with, or exactly where that summer gathering occurred thirty years ago. The only details I remember revolve around the horseshoe tournament my mother participated in.

Mom could not have appeared more different from the Jack she was paired with. She was five feet tall on her tiptoes and weighed 100 pounds post-buffet. Her teammate was a beanstalk, country strong, and looked like he could employ his Popeye forearms to rectify the curve in the horseshoes. I could tell it wasn't his debut by the manner in which he patiently explained the rules to my mom. Because she had never played before, I was expecting an early exit.

But they somehow survived the first round. Then they won again … and again. My mother's partner had a solid game, consistently landing close to the target to score points. Mom, however, was erratic yet displayed homerun potential that would inevitably push her team through to subsequent rounds. Missing the pit entirely at times, she would come back with a clutch leaner against the stake for two points or enring it for three. In fact, it was her final pitch which clinched the title. Her ultimate toss of the competition was actually far short, initially airborne for 30 of the 40 feet to the opposite pole. The metal U she threw nonetheless bounced off the cement preceding the pit in such a way that it was propelled forward, only to be knocked straight down by the stake which it encircled as it came to rest. It was the unlikeliest of ringers, and she was the unlikeliest of champions. Still, the joy she expressed while she jumped up and down made all witnesses happy with the outcome. The last image I recall from that reel was her ear-to-ear grin, which mimicked the shape of the shiny horseshoe displayed atop the trophy she proudly held.

I found myself clutching that trophy three decades later. Packing up her belongings, I uncovered my mom's dusty prize at the bottom of her bedroom closet the day after she succumbed to kidney disease. I reflected upon her incredible run of luck at the tourney. I smiled when thinking of her celebration. I also wondered how I should celebrate her.

Although my father appears in many of my narratives, my mother is present in my stories too—even those which aren't specifically about her. She laid the ground work. In truth, it was a journey with her to the Philippines that sparked my desire to see the world in the first place. And I have kept travelling ever since the two-week trip to her homeland half my life ago. Moreover, Mom could write in her own right. She was quite prolific as it happened, evident in the dense diaries I discovered deep among her possessions. If it wasn't for my mom, I might not have caught the bug which has driven me to explore new parts and meet the people who have made these corners meaningful. If it weren't for her, I may not have been predisposed to record the experiences in the preceding pages. I couldn't have written this book without her. So I dedicate it to her.

Putting together this compilation helped me deal with the void my mother's death left behind. Not only was I able to sort out significant moments, but this process showed me that she and I have a lot more in common than I ever imagined. Elizabeth Acaton Nelson was an extremely giving person, and some of the intangibles she gifted me came to light in the creation of this collection. If not at the forefront, I realized she was behind the scenes of most of these accounts of helping others, hikes down memory lane, healing, and even horseshoes. It turns out I was the lucky one.

Notes

Chapter One—Coming Around to Carnival

Nelson, Tyrel. "Coming Around to Carnival." VIVA Travel Guides, 29 Dec. 2008, http://www.vivatravelguides.com/south-america/ecuador/ecuador-articles/coming-around-to-carnival/.

Chapter Two—Death in Another Light

Nelson, Tyrel. "Seeing death in another light." Travelmag, 17 Jul. 2009, https://www.travelmag.co.uk/2009/07/seeing-death-in-another-light/.

Chapter Three—Views of Vizcaya

Nelson, Tyrel. "Views of Vizcaya." Hackwriters, Dec. 2012, https://www.hackwriters.com/VizcayaTN.htm.

Chapter Four—Flashbacks, Fear, and Flamingos

Nelson, Tyrel. "Flashbacks, Fear, and Flamingos." Hackwriters, Jan. 2013, https://www.hackwriters.com/TNFear.htm.

Chapter Five—Lake Reflections

Nelson, Tyrel. "Lake Reflections." Hackwriters, Oct. 2012, https://www.hackwriters.com/MemoryTN.htm.

Chapter Six—Forging Through the Fourth

Nelson, Tyrel. "Forging Through the Fourth." Hackwriters, Nov. 2012, https://www.hackwriters.com/ForgingTN.htm.

Chapter Seven—Autumn in August

Nelson, Tyrel. "Autumn in August." Hackwriters, Feb. 2013, https://www.hackwriters.com/AutumnTN.htm.

Chapter Eight—February 14

Nelson, Tyrel. "February 14." Hackwriters, Mar. 2013, https://www.hackwriters.com/FarewellTN.htm.

Chapter Nine—The Old Man and the GMC

Nelson, Tyrel. "The Old Man and the GMC." Hackwriters, Apr. 2013, https://www.hackwriters.com/GMCTN.htm.

Chapter Ten—My Takeaway

Nelson, Tyrel. "Here's My Takeaway." Hackwriters, Jun. 2013, https://www.hackwriters.com/TakeawayTN.htm.

Chapter Twelve—Headed for the Devil's Nose

Nelson, Tyrel. "Headed for the Devil's Nose." Hackwriters, Jan. 2017, https://www.hackwriters.com/DevilsNose.htm.

Chapter Thirteen — A Comfortable Silence

Nelson, Tyrel. "A Comfortable Silence." Hackwriters, Mar. 2017, https://www.hackwriters.com/SilenceTN.htm.

Chapter Fourteen — Guatemala Revealed

Nelson, Tyrel. "Guatemala Revealed." In The Know Traveler, 28 Aug. 2020, https://intheknowtraveler.com/guatemala-revealed/.

Nelson, Tyrel. "Guatemala Revealed." Xperitas, 29 Apr. 2020, https://www.xperitas.org/guatemala-revealed. (video journal)

Chapter Fifteen — From 36 to 63

Nelson, Tyrel. "From 36 to 63." Hackwriters, Feb. 2017, https://www.hackwriters.com/RunningTN.htm.

Chapter Sixteen — Looking Back on White Earth

Nelson, Tyrel. "Looking Back on White Earth, Minnesota." In The Know Traveler, 5 Jun. 2020, https://intheknowtraveler.com/looking-back-on-white-earth-minnesota/.

Nelson, Tyrel. "Looking Back on White Earth, Minnesota." Xperitas, 9 Jun. 2020, https://www.xperitas.org/blog/looking-back-on-white-earth-minnesota.

Nelson, Tyrel. "Volunteering at White Earth Reservation." inTravel Magazine, 1 Jul. 2020, https://www.intravelmag.com/intravel/involved/volunteering-at-white-earth-reservation.

Chapter Seventeen — Seven Hours

Nelson, Tyrel. "Seven Hours." Hackwriters, Jun. 2017, https://www.hackwriters.com/7HoursTN.htm.

Chapter Eighteen — Just Before Eight in Central Mexico

Nelson, Tyrel. "Just Before Eight in Central Mexico." In The Know Traveler, 24 Jul. 2020, https://intheknowtraveler.com/just-before-eight-in-central-mexico/.

Chapter Nineteen — Memories of Mom and Mexico

Nelson, Tyrel. "Memories of My Mother and Mexico." Hackwriters, 1 Aug. 2020, https://www.hackwriters.com/Memories2TN.htm.

Other Works by Tyrel Nelson

Stories from Ecuador: A Collection by Tyrel Nelson

Stories from Ecuador is a collection of honest, first-hand accounts of the most memorable people, places, and moments from a young man's year-long journey in Latin America. Tyrel Nelson's prose breathes life into the characters he befriends along the way and sketches  scenes with the telescopic perspective that one only gains by stepping outside the American mainstream. Setting off from Quito to begin his training to teach English (TESOL), you tag along traversing the Ecuadorian countryside surrounding Cuenca as Nelson documents his experiences and transformation from a Minnesota native into a true citizen of the world. Using the rich landscape as the backdrop for his stories, he not only shows a keen eye for cultural and historical detail, but an artist's flare for blending personal perspective with the attributes of a solid narrative. From the encounters with his quirky landlord and neighbors in Cuenca to quixotic adventures with his brother, Nelson serves up a colorful mix of tales incorporating levity, beauty and even boredom, in an unexpected and refreshing way.
—Daniel Patrick Holmay

Those Darn Stripes

In his third book, Tyrel Nelson offers a patchwork of lovingly constructed vignettes that  interweave themes of change, loss, and joy, all while managing to preserve a light-hearted and inspiring tone. Written in straightforward and sparse language, his narratives touch upon the impact of fleeting interpersonal encounters as well as the enduring effect of past and present relationships. Throughout his short collection of stories, Nelson's prose deepens and matures to mirror the effect that significant life changes have had upon his emotional psyche. Through his prose, seemingly ordinary journeys become powerful stories that engagingly transform the banality of quotidian encounters into opportunities for remarkable life transformations. These moving stories are both touching and inspiring. They are not easily forgotten, as they speak to the essence of our human community. —Andra Bosneag

Made in the USA
Monee, IL
29 July 2021